THE
GUARLFORD SCENE

Also by the Guarlford History Group

The Guarlford Story

Published in 2005

THE
GUARLFORD SCENE

Don Hill
Eric Jones
Janet Lomas
Peter Mayner
Angus McCulloch
Rosemary McCulloch
Michael Skinner

The Guarlford History Group

Published in the United Kingdom, 2008, by
The Guarlford History Group
4 Bamford Close
Guarlford
Malvern
WR13 6PF

ISBN 978-0-9550498-1-1

Book design, layout and photograph restoration by Michael Skinner.

Printed in England by
Print Plus
126 Widemarsh Street
Hereford
HR4 9HN

DEDICATION

This book is dedicated to the parishioners of Guarlford, past and present, both those who are seen or are mentioned in this history and also the many more who have spent all or part of their lives in this small Worcestershire village.

THE AUTHORS

Donald J Hill.   Don was born in Richmond, Yorkshire. After leaving school, he enlisted in the army as an apprentice and then went on to serve as soldier and electronics engineer in the Royal Electrical and Mechanical Engineers (REME) until retirement in the rank of major in 1991. In 1979, while working at the REME establishment in Malvern, he and his wife Barbara came to live in Guarlford, but did not take up permanent residence until 1986. For many years, he has been treasurer, then churchwarden to Guarlford Church and Chairman of the Village Hall Committee. Past activities include Village Fete organiser, Madresfield Parish Clerk and Madresfield School Governor. He is also treasurer to the Malvern branches of two Service charities, SSAFA Forces Help and the Royal British Legion.

Dr Eric H Jones.   Born in Oxford and brought up in Cardiff, Eric was educated at three universities, including the University of Texas, U.S.A. His interest in American literature led to the award in 1973 of a Ph.D. for a thesis on the poetry and fiction of Sylvia Plath, completed with essential moral and typing support from his wife, Siti. They both came to live in Guarlford in 1976 for Eric to take up appointment as Head of English and Drama at what is now the University of Worcester in January, 1977. In the mid-1990s he made a career move to become the first Director of Worcester's International Office. Subsequent visits overseas on behalf of both the university and the British Council included destinations in China, India, Malaysia, the U.S.A., and various European countries. Committed to Guarlford as a community over many years since the Silver Jubilee of 1977, he has been actively involved as a Parish Councillor and in other ways for more than twenty-five years. Wider interests include international travel, the countryside – especially National Parks – the National Trust, and art history.

Janet Lomas.   Janet and her husband farm the Home Farm of the Madresfield Estate, farming both sides of the Madresfield and Guarlford parish boundary. Her interest in local history began at home, where there is a wealth of historic interest and archaeological features. Janet has been Guarlford Parish Council's appointed tree warden for eight years, and is a keen wildlife conservationist, working both as a local volunteer for several national and local organisations and also as a full-time farm conservation adviser with the Herefordshire Farming and Wildlife Advisory Group (FWAG). As well as advising farmers on wildlife conservation, her work with FWAG involves promoting conservation of the historic landscape.

Dr Peter E Mayner.   Peter has lived all his life within the original Guarlford parish boundary and for the last fifty-one years at Cherry Orchard. Educated at Haileybury College, the original East India Company's college, and then Trinity College, Cambridge, and Birmingham University, where he studied medicine, he also gained his Royal Air Force Volunteer Reserve wings with the Birmingham University Air Squadron. He developed an interest in underwater archaeology through founding membership of scuba diving clubs at the two universities. Peter worked in local hospitals after qualifying, prior to joining the Peninsular and Oriental Steam Navigation Company. Extensive travel around the world culminated in service 'under fire' as Company Medical Officer in the Falklands Conflict when the 'SS Canberra' was requisitioned. After twenty years at sea, he was forced by ill health to retire home to Guarlford, where he is Chairman of the Parish Council, a member of the committee and a past Chairman of the English Symphony Orchestra's 'Friends'; he also pursues interests which include music, the National Trust, rugby, cricket and wine-making!

Angus McCulloch.   Angus was born in Surrey. He obtained a degree in Electronic Engineering at the University of Wales, Bangor, in 1966 and joined the Scientific Civil Service working for the Signals Research and Development Establishment at Christchurch (SRDE). In 1978, the family moved to Malvern when SRDE was amalgamated with the Royal Radar Establishment to form the Royal Signals and Radar Establishment. Angus enjoyed a varied career working on communications and computer-based projects before retiring in 2006. He now maintains the Guarlford Web Site for the Guarlford History Group.

Rosemary McCulloch.   Rosemary moved to Malvern in 1978, when her husband Angus transferred to the Royal Signals and Radar Establishment from the Signals Research and Development Establishment, Christchurch. Their three sons attended Madresfield School, where Rosemary served as a Parent Governor, and she also helped the Reverend David Martin to start the Ben-efice Junior Church in 1982. She has an Honours degree in English from the University of Wales, Bangor, and, after being Supervisor of Lansdowne Play-group, taught in Malvern, mainly at the Chase High School, as a supply teacher for many years. With many interests, mostly concerned with family and community life - topics which she enjoyed researching for the present book - Rosemary was also President of Guarlford Women's Institute from November 1998 to 2007.

J Michael Skinner.   After completing National Service in the Royal Signals, Michael came to Malvern in 1952 to join the Radar Research and Development Establishment at Leigh Sinton. He remained with the establishment through its many amalgamations and name changes until he retired in 1990 from full-time service from what had become the Royal Signals and Radar Establishment. He continued working part-time to represent the UK on both the Steering Committee and Project Management Board of an international NATO research project on automated Information Fusion and Visualisation. This was a particularly rewarding time as it involved visiting and working with very friendly and co-operative scientists and engineers from Canada, Denmark, France, Germany, Italy and the Netherlands. He finally retired in 2000, after the successful completion of the project. Michael moved to Guarlford with his family in 1971 and became involved in village life as Secretary to the Silver Jubilee Committee, Secretary and Trustee of the Village Hall, and, from 1980, Parish Clerk.

ACKNOWLEDGEMENTS

The authors are deeply indebted to the Local Heritage Initiative (LHI) whose advice and grant, supplemented with the proceeds from the sale of the first book, *The Guarlford Story*, have made possible the creation and publication of this, the Guarlford History Group's second book, *The Guarlford Scene*.

The Local Heritage Initiative is a national grant scheme that helps local groups to investigate, explain and care for their landscape, traditions and culture. The LHI was developed by the Countryside Agency, but is now managed by the Heritage Lottery Fund (HLF) and funded by the HLF and the Nationwide Building Society.

This book could not have been written without the help and enthusiasm of the present and former parishioners of Guarlford who not only agreed to be interviewed but who also searched out and made available their old family photographs, and gave permission for both their accounts of Guarlford village life and their family and other photographs to be included in this book. The authors would like to express their thanks to all these contributors for their invaluable help and apologise if anyone has been omitted or if there are any inadvertent inaccuracies in the accounts.

The authors would also like to record their appreciation for the help provided by the Worcester Record Office and the Worcestershire Historic Environment and Archaeology Service, and to thank the following for permission to reproduce their photographs: the Defence Science and Technology Laboratories (Dstl), MOD; Newsquest (Midlands South); the *Malvern Gazette*; Berrows Newspapers; Norman May, Photographer, and Mrs J Preece for C D Walton's photographs.

The front cover illustration is from a photograph by Mr C D Walton showing Mr Bladder striking a deal. The Foley Estate Map, a portion of which is shown on page xiv, was kindly presented to the History Group by Mrs Layton, whose husband was a partner in Harper and Layton, the Estate Agents. The photograph of the authors on the back cover is by Newsquest.

Although every attempt has been taken to establish the provenance of the photographs published in this book, it has not always been possible, especially in the case of very old photographs, to determine whether the copyright is actually owned by the provider (who has provided permission) or a third party or has indeed expired. The authors apologise if, by mischance, a copyright photograph has been included without the owner's permission. Where known, the attribution and copyright for each photograph is included in its caption.

Contributors

Mr H Ashford,
Mr C Attwood,
Mrs P Bayliss,
Mr M Beard,
Mr S G Beard,
Mr F Beard,
Mrs M Bennett,
Mr R Bevan,
Mrs D Bick,
Mrs M Birkett,
Mr D Bladder,
Mr H Bladder,
Mrs P Bladder,
Mr G Bott,
Mrs J Bott,
Miss J Bradshaw,
Mr J Bradshaw,
Mr D Brickell,
Mr K Chester,

Mrs J Clark,
Mrs J M Crisp,
Mr N Deam,
Mrs C E Dring,
Mrs E Dunn,
Mrs P Fairhurst,
Mr J Gammond,
Mrs L Gilroy,
Mr R Gilroy,
Mrs J Guest,
Mrs J Hadley-Roberts,
Mr C Hayes,
Mrs D Hayes,
Mr D Hewins,
Mr D Hill,
Mr P Hughes,
Mr B Hulme,
Mrs M Hunaban,
Mr C Hyde,

Mr B Iles,
Mr E Jenkins,
Mrs J Kershaw,
Miss P Jones,
Mr E Lane,
Mr D Lawson,
Mr C Lettice,
Mr J Little,
Mrs E Llewelyn,
Mrs C Lockley,
Mrs J Lomas,
Dr P E Mayner,
Mr A Medcalf,
Mrs E Medcalf,
Mr A McCulloch,
Mrs R McCulloch,
Mrs R McCarry,
Mr S Micklethwait,
Miss C Moody,

Miss J Newell,
Mr M Peach,
Plough and Harrow,
Mrs M Omar,
Mr C Roberts,
Mr K Rickards,
Mrs M Rutter,
Mr K Shinn,
Mr J M Skinner,
Mr M Simpson,
Mr K Tandy,
Mrs M R Thomas,
Mrs S Thorne,
Mr A Tummey,
Mr T Vivian,
Mr P Titchener,
Mrs M Waldron,
Mr J R Walker,
Mrs J Ward,

Mr H Webb,
Mrs C Weaver,
Mrs S Wheeler,
Mr J A Whitlock,
Mr M Wilks,
Mr C R Williams,
Mrs R Williams,
Mr E Williams,
Mr K Woolley,
Sir Jerry Wiggin,
Mr B Wyndham,
Mr A Young,
Mrs O Young,
Mr J Young,
Commander Ratcliff's
grandchildren.

Supported by
The National Lottery®
through the Heritage Lottery Fund

Heritage
Lottery Fund

FOREWORD

The previous book, *The Guarlford Story*, published in 2005, has sold well over 700 copies to date, an encouraging testimony to the interest there is in the history of the village, an interest which has greatly encouraged the authors in their work on the present publication. As promised in *The Guarlford Story*, the Guarlford History Group continues to create an archive of material, especially photographs and interviews, to enlarge the record of the village's twentieth and twenty-first century life.

The Guarlford Scene thus builds upon earlier work while at the same time providing a self-contained and more pictorial account of the recent past. Our intention in creating this book has also been to bring the picture up-to-date by including photographs of the village and its inhabitants today, so that future historians can see the way we were just a few years into a new century.

It is the hope of the authors that in the future Guarlfordians will be stimulated by the two books we have published to expand the story and the scene by adding memories and photographs to the existing store and do so, not least, by making use of the Guarlford Website at any time.

I do hope you will enjoy our book and find much to interest you and to reflect upon.

Dr P E Mayner

Chairman
Guarlford Parish Council

Bluebell Wood, Dripshill by Pat Lowry.

CONTENTS

The Church Bell by Tom Vivian.

GARFORD COURT

belonging to Berkleys Hospital
in the CITY of WORCESTER

Blaney
Esq.

GEORGE

NEED

Leigh Parish

Mr Samuel Roe

Mr William Bullock

John
Barber

To the Rhydd, and Upton

GREEN

Garford Court

Mr William Bullock Junr

Mrs Hannah Ebb

Mrs Wilson

The Cherry Orchard

GEORGE

Malvern Church Land

JOHN BEARD

NEED

Mrs Wilson

George Lane
Woodbridge

GEORGE

Court

NEED

Mr George Need

Garford

ROBERTS

STREET

WOOD

LEY

CASTLE

The Property of Thomas Charles Hornyold Esquire

A MAP

of several ESTATES

situate in the Parish, and forming the Manor

OF

GREAT · MALVERN,

In the County of

WORCESTER

The Property of Edward, Thomas Foley Esq.

Scale of Chains

10   0   10   20   30   40

INTRODUCTION

"... history is a pattern/ Of timeless moments."

T S Eliot

This book is a collection of photographs of the Worcestershire village of Guarlford. The photographs record moments in the lives of individuals, families and groups from 1900 to the present day, as well as portraying buildings, farms, businesses and landscape features which make up the local scene. A great variety of cameras, held usually by unknown persons, have captured "timeless moments" and done so without any foreknowledge in most cases of publication in a book such as this many years later. The photographers were, in a sense, making history without realising it.

The Guarlford scene is set historically by the map showing estates as they were in 1828 before some significant additions and changes, with only a handful of buildings indicated, most notably 'Garford Court', but with field boundaries and ownership clearly marked.

Between the two World Wars, a series of county books by Arthur Mee was published, namely *The King's England*, and the books have become classics of their kind. Each offers a vivid and atmospheric guide to the towns and villages of a particular county. A distinguishing feature of Mee's style is his powerful sense of his-

tory, while each volume, including the one on Worcestershire, also contains superb black and white photographs. Of Guarlford, Mee says it "... lies on a beautiful road, with wide green verges, which runs straight across the flat meadows from Rhydd, near the Severn, to the heart of Malvern. It is a small, scattered village, and the church is Victorian, as are so many in this part of the county." p.90 This simple, straightforward evocation of Guarlford in the Worcestershire landscape is no less apt today than it was when it was written. Guarlford would still be recognisable to Mee; it is to this day "... a small, scattered village" and the "... beautiful road, with wide green verges" still provides the village with a setting to enjoy and be proud of.

The photographs of this village and of the people who have made their lives here over generations are photographs capturing moments in time in the history of one among ten thousand or more English villages. There is perhaps a "pattern" to be discerned in the repetitions and continuities of the lives that have been lived here - the births, the marriages, and other defining moments in human experience. Of course, there will often be many specific memories and associations attached to photographs, and for those who know or knew people seen in the pages which follow some of those memories will be happy or amusing, while others will occasionally be sad. For readers less acquainted with the village, this book will provide a broad introduction to the Guarlford scene and what is unique about it, for every English place is different, no matter how much is shared with a wider world.

At the centre of any village community there are certain families and their descendants who have played a dominant and even shaping role in the making of the place and its distinctive character. Farming and rural businesses are, of course, self-evidently important in defining the nature of this corner of historic England. The experiences which the older members of the village community recall are often bound up with agriculture in some way and also with the horses which shared the hard work with the men in the fields, those horses also providing a unique kind of companionship. Charlie Williams, in particular, bears witness to this.

The twentieth century will forever be defined to a very large extent by the experience of the two World Wars which had an impact on every family in the land. In the 1940s, Guarlford had its Home Guard and its evacuees, and it still has its 'Listening Post'. As can be seen in the account of several family histories, in both the First and the Second World War individual members proudly wore the uniform of all three major services, as well as that of the Land Army, while more recent conflicts have also taken Guarlfordians to places far from home.

Until the last thirty or so years, there was a vigorous and diverse community life in the village, as in most English villages. It was evidenced, for example, in the Guarlford Football Club and its regular matches throughout the season, while in a different way the small shops and other rural businesses also helped to bring people together. Small, family-owned village stores, in particular, have typically provided opportunities for the exchange of local news and gossip; sadly, none remains in Guarlford now. Other than the church, however, no village institution or organisation mattered more than the village school, where generations of children shared a common experience and many life-long friendships were formed. The class photographs collected in this book show successive groups of Guarlford children over the years, many of whom were to grow up and spend their entire lives in the village, often recalling school days as very happy ones – something which is a tribute, not least, to their teachers. The closure of Guarlford School shortly after the end of the Second World War meant that this most important source of both village identity and village social cohesion no longer existed; while, at the same time, other factors such as greater mobility by means of the private motor car and the advent of television mass entertainment have also contributed, as they have everywhere, to the considerable loss of a shared sense of place.

In spite of changes and some significant losses, there is much that continues to make Guarlford a distinctive community and one which has pride in itself. St Mary's still provides a regular place of worship, as well as helping to sustain a crucial sense of continuity with the past. The Women's Institute thrives and makes an invaluable contribution to the village. It regularly assists local social life by providing refreshments at various occasions, including presentations and events put on by the Guarlford History Group. One such occasion was held on 24th January, 2008, when Mr Charlie

Williams gave a talk to a large audience in the Village Hall, a vivid account of Guarlford life in the twentieth century seen through the eyes of someone who had witnessed it first-hand. This occasion was itself another memorable moment in Guarlford history. The earlier celebrations of the two royal Jubilees and the Millennium year were also especially significant and memorable occasions. Similarly, the Local Heritage Initiative and Heritage Lottery-funded History Project has, since 2002, brought villagers together in shared community endeavour and pride. It was a pride manifested, too, when Guarlford achieved an award in Worcestershire's 'Community Pride' competition five years ago as recognition of the successful restoration of the village pond and our beautifully maintained churchyard. The appearance of the village environment is important, and efforts are constantly and rightly made to keep it tidy and attractive.

Photographs of neighbourhood groups at the end of *The Guarlford Scene* help to bring the record up to date and serve as a reminder that this "small, scattered village" has a relatively large population, the majority of whom have taken the opportunity to become part of this permanent historical record. It is worth noting that there are quite a number of comparative newcomers in these photographs, 'newcomers' who not only exemplify the mobility of people characteristic of the second half of the twentieth century, but who also, and more importantly, represent a readiness to play their part in maintaining village life and identity.

What used to be a natural part of the warp and weft of village life now has to be worked for more deliberately: those who care about local history and identity must seek, as far as possible, to fill the gap left by the disappearance of the village school, the football club, the village shops and more besides.

If, as the poet T S Eliot wrote, "...history is a pattern/Of timeless moments", then many such moments for Guarlford are captured by the photographs in this book. Whether a studio portrait, a family or other group photograph or a more casual 'snap', the click of a shutter has converted a transitory moment into something permanent and 'timeless'. The exact date of a photograph may not be recorded in all or even many cases, let alone the hour or minute, but the pattern of such timeless moments creates a picture that is larger than the individual image. It is the pattern of Guarlford life in the twentieth and early twenty-first century brought to life in print so that, again in T.S.Eliot's words, "History is now and England".

Quotations are from: T S Eliot, 'Little Gidding', one of the 'Four Quartets', *The Complete Poems and Plays of T S Eliot*, Faber, 1969, p.197; and Arthur Mee, *The King's England Worcestershire*, Hodder and Stoughton, 1968.

Chapter 1

The Families of Guarlford

Introduction

The story of Guarlford is essentially a history of village families, and the photographs reproduced in this book portray families and a way of life during a period of just over one hundred years. A relatively small number of families have been at the heart of Guarlford's life during this time and most of them can be seen in the pages which follow. In a rural setting, it is to be expected that the farming families will play a particularly prominent part, while the way of life is one which often reflects the farming year, its work and occasional leisure, as was seen also in *The Guarlford Story*. But at a more fundamental level what is evident is the enduring importance of family bonds over generations, with young and old often pictured together at some of the key moments of life – the family gatherings and special occasions when those ties and loyalties were expressed and reinforced.

The twentieth century saw two World Wars and, like families the length and breadth of Britain, Guarlford families were brought even closer together. Indeed, the whole village community might be said to have been brought together as one family in a common cause. It was a cause which also brought hardship, uncertainty and anxiety, as well as desperate concern for those in uniform and away from home. War-time meant separation, but, paradoxically, it also meant that people were closer together as they shared the same testing ordeal. There is a kind of added intensity to human experience in time of World War that perhaps offsets to some small extent its darker side.

A number of Guarlford families, families sharing ties, loyalties, history and identity, have lived in the village for generations and on into the twentieth century, when war brought its own strengthening of bonds. It is also true that the village history of the last fifty or so years has seen something of the same fragmentation and dispersal of families to other parts of the country or overseas which has characterised family life throughout Britain. In addition, our mobile society has seen residents with no previous Guarlford history arrive to settle in the village. The continuities and the closeness of

Cider Press at Woodbridge Farm by Barbara Hill.

family life are no longer what they were, and the same might be said of village life as a whole.

There are twenty Guarlford families here representing their generations of life in this village and, at the same time, something of the history of the place itself: the Bartleet/Mayners; the Bayliss/Bedingtons; the Beards; the Bradshaws; the Gillett Burtons; the Bladders; the Hayes/Clarkes; the Pantings; the Lanes; the Littles; the Medcalfs; the Newsons; the Shinns; the Smiths; the Vivians; the Whitlocks; and the Williamses. In addition, there are Lane and Panting family trees; and these might be seen, not least, as illustrative of what is possible for families who have at least one family member willing to undertake the necessary work. Interest in family histories and family trees has never been greater than at the present time, an interest encouraged by a range of available resources and the greater access to records provided by the Internet. Undoubtedly, too, the current interest is quickened by the sense that a world we have otherwise lost is still just recoverable through fading photographs, as well as memories, that can be restored and published with greater permanence. While not every long-established Guarlford family is to be seen in the photographs, and the authors have, as always, depended on the photographs and information that have been made available, the whole picture in this chapter is a substantial and varied one, a cross-section of people, occupations, occasions and the generations. The details, of necessity, may be fragmentary, but there is a rich story told in these photographs for everyone with the interest and imagination to follow it.

The images capture moments in Guarlford family life with a deliberation no longer to be seen in our digital age. Taking a photograph used to be much more of an event and there was a sense of occasion about it, even if it was just a 'snap'. The recent group photographs in the 'Neighbourhood Groups' section later in *The Guarlford Scene* have something of this quality, but they were taken for the book, not for a family occasion or village event as such.

There is a story told here, then, or a series of stories, albeit a necessarily very incomplete one, of Guarlford families and how they were different – not least in each individual family's likeness in physical appearance over generations – and also of what they had in common living in one place at one time. Here are moments from the past given renewed life and meaning, we hope, in print.

The outline map opposite locates the family homes of the families represented in this chapter and also helps to set the scene for this pictorial sequel to *The Guarlford Story*.

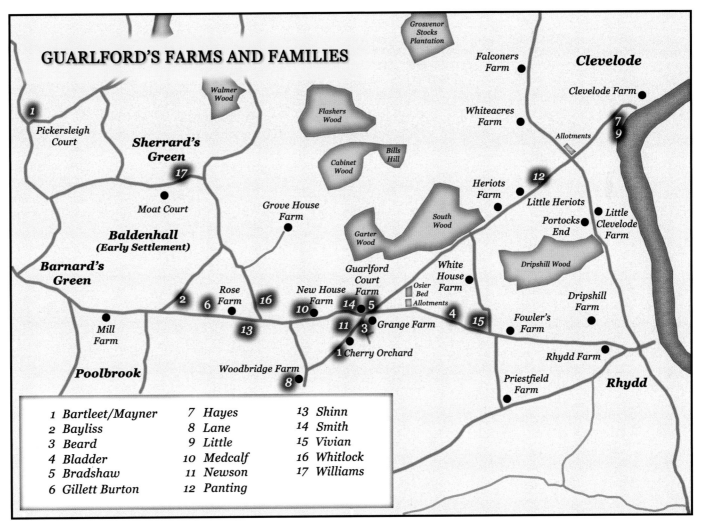

Figure 1.1 The Farms and Families of Guarlford.

The Bartleet and Mayner Families

Robert and Lucie Bartleet (6) and their family came to Cherry Orchard in 1957 from Pickersleigh Court, in the northwest of the original ecclesiastical parish, where they had spent the early years of their married life. Pickersleigh Court had belonged to Robert's family until it was sold to the Madresfield Estate in 1910 to pay death duties on his grandfather's estate.

Robert's grandparents were Sir Henry and Lady Foley Lambert (7), whose family donated the land upon which St Mary's, our village church, was built. Sir Henry was one of those instrumental in setting up the Malvern Council, and was also a founder of the Malvern Hills Conservators.

Robert (2) was an artist and horse-lover, who hunted with the Croome Hunt from the 1920s to the 1960s. He was also a long-standing Malvern Hills Conservator and served on Guarlford Parish Council. He may also be seen in *The Guarlford Story* on p. 173 at a presentation made in 1991 to long-serving Parish Councillors.

Lucie (1) was a great animal lover who bred dachshunds. She was the widow of Albert Mayner, an engineer whose father had founded the first Motor Bus Company in Birmingham, converting his horse-drawn carriages in the early 1900s. (Albert senior was a friend and sometime partner of Herbert Austin, who bought land at Longbridge from Robert Bartleet's family for his motor factory.) On the loss of her second husband in the Second World War, Lucie moved to Malvern with her two young children, Carole and Peter, where she met and married Robert Bartleet. Humphrey, their son, a successful local businessman who has a wholesale kitchenware import business, lives at Longdon Heath with his wife and three sons. He is pictured (5) with his father and Dr Peter Mayner setting off for the Madresfield Show, which Robert helped to restart after the Second World War at the invitation of the 8th (and last) Earl Beauchamp.

Dr Peter and Elizabeth Mayner are pictured (3) on their honeymoon in 1977 on board 'SS Oriana' in the South Pacific, when Peter was Company Medical Officer with the Peninsular and Oriental Steam Navigation Company. He is also a RAF Reserve Pilot, and he served as Senior Surgeon in 'SS Canberra' during the Falklands Conflict of 1982. They live at Cherry Orchard with their daughter, Rebecca, and grandson, Rio. Peter is at present Chairman of Guarlford Parish Council, while he also gives considerable support to Malvern's musical life as well as local activities such as Guarlford history research.

Carole Mayner (4) married the singer Danny Williams, famous for his Golden Disc 'Moon River', the theme from the 1961 Audrey Hepburn film, *Breakfast at Tiffany's*. She has one daughter and several grandchildren.

Figure 1.2 The Mayner Bartleet Montage.

The Bayliss Family

Mrs Phyl Bayliss was born Phyl Bedington on May 26th, 1916, the very day on which her father commenced his army service in the First World War. Phyl and her two brothers, Stanley and John, lived with their parents in a cottage at Hall Green, where 'The Paddocks' now stands. In about 1922, Phyl is seen (2) on the left in the garden with her cousin, Evelyn Bedington. In the adjacent Jackpit Lane stood a thatched cottage (1) where lived Phyl's great grandparents, Enoch and Anne Pearce (nee Weston), who worked at Madresfield Court. Phyl also remembered Jackpit Lane full of gypsy caravans, and the gypsies coming to obtain water from the Bedington's pump.

Phyl grew up surrounded by fields and common land; she and other members of the Bedington and Williams families took advantage of this and had picnics on Hall Green common (6).

In the Second World War, Phyl became a Land Girl (3) and worked on the Guinness Hop Farm at Braces Leigh for three years; and later she worked as a switchboard operator at the American Army Hospital at Blackmore Camp.

After the War, on a snowy January 21st, 1946, Phyl married Owen Bayliss, whom she met when he was playing football for Guarlford, and, as Owen worked for Mr Bakewell of Grove House Farm, they then lived for twenty-nine years in a cottage off Chance Lane.

Phyl and Owen (on the far left) can be seen (5) at the Guarlford Fete in 1953: the children are: (back row) Wendy White, Annette Read, Gordon Beauchamp and Philip Bayliss as a pirate; (front row) Pat Tainton, Rosemary Beale as 'a doll in a box', Beryl Dewey as a fairy, Madie Bayliss as 'Little Bo-peep', and Terry Bedington.

Phyl's skills as a needlewoman were well-known. She once came third in a Women's Institute County Craft Class with an exquisite rag doll called 'Topsy'; and people in the parish still recall the dolls Phyl made and dressed as presents at Christmas.

Phyl remembered vividly how happy she was at Guarlford School with her best and life-long friend Rene Sims and others. Rene's garden near the Village Hall was the setting for a group photograph (4): (standing) Joan Bradshaw, Jo Newell, Phyl Bayliss and Thelma Ackerman (once of 'The Tan House'), with (seated) Rene Sims and Mrs Newson, widow of the Revd Newson.

In 2006, Phyl celebrated her 90th birthday, and her first great grandchild named Owen Bayliss was born. Phyl's achievement in her ninety-first year was being able to attend his christening in February 2007. She died suddenly and very peacefully on Tuesday 27th March, 2007.

Figure 1.3 The Bayliss Montage.

The Beard Family

According to Samuel George Thomas Beard (Sam), born in 1920, the Beards first "... came off the river, landed at Clevelode and looked round for somewhere to live, came across 'The Noggin', which was deserted, and moved in." It is recorded that a Thomas Beard, born about 1762, lived at Rhydd. Sam's grandfather, George Edward Beard, born in 1873 at a cottage in Portock's End, is seen with his mother, Elizabeth, and sisters, Sarah (later Scriven), Alice (later Wells) and Elizabeth (later Hemming), around 1900 (1).

George Edward Beard was a well-known personality in Guarlford and can be seen with his wife Rosina (6) in the 1920s and at a Guarlford village fete in 1937-8 (2). His working life was spent on farms, the roads, and even putting in the clay to line the reservoir at British Camp, constructed in 1892, walking there daily from Guarlford. George devoted his life to the village in many ways, including faithfully serving the church, where he was verger for thirty-seven years. He was also a server, bellringer and gravedigger. He tidied the churchyard, lit the boiler and the lamps every week before electricity arrived – he was seen as the Revd F Newson's 'right-hand man'. His wife, Rosina, cared for the church linen and vestments, which were laundered to a high standard.

The family lived for many years at Malthouse Cottage, where the group photograph (5) was taken during the First World War. Pictured here are: Jim Probert, Royal Artillery, with his wife, Lizzie, (nee Beard) and daughter Mary; Jack Beard, Oxford and Bucks, and George Beard, Royal Artillery, standing behind their father George E Beard, Worcestershire Volunteers, their mother, Rosina, and Samuel T. Beard, Rifle Brigade, with his wife, Emily.

Sam, son of Samuel and Emily Beard, recalls that an annual event during his childhood was the arrival of a Royal Artillery unit from South Wales, which camped at Blackmore Park and carried out exercises on the broad Guarlford commons. Seeing these exercises, and hearing the tales of his father and uncles from the First World War, encouraged Sam to join the Territorial Army in 1938, which meant that he was mobilised two days before the Second World War began. He was in a reserved occupation as a baker in Malvern Link, but he chose to join the army with his friends. During the Second World War, Sam served in Britain, Iceland, North Western Europe and India.

Sam and his wife, Freda, are seen on their wedding day in 1941 (3). While Sam was on a short embarkation leave, the couple needed a special licence to marry in the time available; and so Sam cycled not only to see the clergy of Guarlford and Holy Trinity, but also to the Old Palace in Worcester to collect the licence.

In October 2006, Sam and Freda celebrated their sixty-fifth wedding anniversary at a party in Guarlford Village Hall (4).

Figure 1.4 The Beard Montage.

The Bladder Family

In 1924, Cooper Bladder moved with his family from Winyates Farm, near Redditch, to Guarlford to work for his father at Fowler's Farm. The farm was famous for its stallions, and Mr Cooper Bladder is holding the reins of 'Dripshill Bob', sometime in the 1930s (1). The little boy riding the stallion is Les Bentley. In the 1939 season, 'Dripshill Forest King' was pictured as "The Property of H.C. Bladder", an excellent Shire stallion, and is to be seen in *The Guarlford Story* (p. 21).

Cooper's full name was Laud William Cooper Bladder. Cooper's older brother, Theodore Henry Charles Hawkins Bladder, (2) served with the Royal Navy during the First World War and was at the Battle of Jutland.

Cooper and Florence had four sons: Charles, Derrick, Wallace and Reginald. Charles, born in 1920, with Thelma Ackermann and her grandmother, Mrs (Granny) Thomas, stands outside 'Tan House', next to the 'Plough and Harrow' in Guarlford (7). Mrs Thomas ran the little sweet and tobacco shop there.

The Bladder family lived at 'The Glen', Rhydd Road, and were gathered there in the Second World War (4), and are seen from left to right: Reginald, Wallace, Cousin Gwen, Derrick, Mrs Florence Mabel Bladder, together with an unidentified evacuee. American soldiers convalescing at Blackmore Park came across the fields from the camp for the cups of tea and cake provided by Mrs Bladder on her lawn.

As the Second World War approached, Charles joined the Territorial Army, and when war was declared in 1939, although he was only nineteen, he was immediately called up. He joined the Royal Artillery and was sent to France as part of the British Expeditionary Force. The telegram (3) was sent by Charles when he returned safely from Dunkirk in 1940; he had escaped on the 'Ivanhoe', which, half way back across the English Channel, was hit by a bomb just in front of the front funnel, killing forty men. Charles was at the rear of the ship, which managed to limp back to England.

After Dunkirk, Charles was sent to Egypt and fought with the Eighth Army under General Montgomery, taking part in the Battle of El-Alamein of October- November, 1942 - a true 'Desert Rat'. Charles was in Ismailia, Egypt, on the evening of August 15th, 1942, (6). In 1944, he was "mentioned in Despatches" for distinguished service.

Derrick Bladder joined the RAF in 1942 and was involved in the 1944 'D-Day' preparations. He spent two years in France, and (5) shows Derrick (on the left) in 1946.

Figure 1.5 The Bladder Montage.

The Bradshaw Family

The 1891 Census returns show that Absalom Bradshaw and his family (1), who later became prominent members of the Guarlford community, were at that time living in Davenham Cottage, Malvern. On the far right is Absalom, standing with his elder son, also named Absalom but known as 'Abbie', who was born in 1873, and daughter, Violet Mary, born in 1874. Seated is their mother, Mary A. Bradshaw, with a young Oliver Victor George Bradshaw, born in 1887, sitting on her lap. Absalom had brought his family to Malvern from Buckinghamshire, where he had been employed as garden designer at Waddesdon Manor, regarded as having one of the finest Victorian gardens in Britain. Absalom put his design skills to use planning and laying out Davenham's gardens while living there.

Young Abbie's diary for 1894 mentions his experience as a bell-ringer at the Priory in Great Malvern.

In 1898, the Bradshaws moved to Guarlford Court, and so began a long association with Guarlford. The family is shown in a photograph taken around 1900 (2). Abbie and Victor stand behind their father, sister Violet, and mother. Abbie, to be seen on the Guarlford Court Farm Dairy cart (6), eventually moved to Cheshire to farm on his own.

In 1913, Victor, known as 'O.V.G.' in the records of many village societies, married Florence Ada Price, also of Guarlford. Florence was at that time an assistant teacher with Mrs Martin at Guarlford National School (see Chapter 3). Victor and Florence then farmed White House Farm as tenants, where their daughter, Joan Violet, was born on June 28th, 1918. The couple then moved to Guarlford Court (3) to take over the tenancy from Absalom senior.

Victor's and Florence's son, Colin John Kenelm, was born in 1919, and so was just twenty years of age when the Second World War began. He is pictured in his uniform (4) as a RAF pilot with his wife, Peggy (nee Featherstone), whom he married in February, 1944.

The Bradshaws lived at Guarlford Court until about 1935, and then at Grange Farm, so that the young Joan grew up in the centre of village life and close to the church. The stories and history of the village fascinated Joan, and she was a true historian, recording all she was told about Guarlford. Her painstaking research was an invaluable source and inspiration for the Guarlford History Group and for *The Guarlford Story*, as well as this book. Joan, with her friend Joan (Jo) Newell, was the guest of honour at the launch party for *The Guarlford Story* on a memorable day in August, 2005, at Cherry Orchard (5).

Figure 1.6 The Bradshaw Montage 1.

Joan Bradshaw

Joan Bradshaw spent most of a long and fulfilled life in Guarlford. She left the village to train at Sutton Bonnington Agricultural College in Nottinghamshire (8), and in the Second World War served in the Women's Land Army for Mr Tolley at Lower Woodsfield Farm, near Madresfield, during which time she received five commendation badges, one of which is shown (7), together with a letter of congratulations.

Joan's greatest joy was working with animals, especially horses, and she was a successful point-to-pointer, particularly with 'Robin Adair'. Joan can be seen (9) with another favourite, 'Donegal'.

Victor Bradshaw had bought Grange Farm, and after the Second World War Joan set up a small livestock farm there with her friend, Jo Newell, shown in (10) driving their Riley, nicknamed 'Barkis'. They kept dairy cows, sheep and pigs, and bred hunters. When they could no longer manage livestock farming, the two Joans founded Grange Farm Nursery, which has continued to flourish since Carol Nicholls bought it in 1980. Indeed, on the very day of Joan's funeral in 2007, it was announced that Grange Farm Nursery had won an RHS Gold medal at the Spring Garden Show held at the Three Counties Ground, Malvern.

At the funeral service to celebrate Joan's life, Meriel Bennett described the familiar sight of Joan "... on a summer's day in one of her trade-mark floral skirts and a wide-brimmed straw hat, trug on her arm, and one of her beloved dachshunds at her heel ..." tending the garden or cutting flowers for St Mary's Church.

Joan's final journey to the church she attended so often and which was so dear to her heart took place on the 10th May, 2007. Belinda James of Priestfield's Farm gently guided the carriage carrying Joan's coffin right to the church door (1.9). As well as the family floral tributes, the carriage was covered with flowers from Joan's garden at Grange Farm, and among those following Joan on her last journey to the church she loved so much can be seen Rosemary McCarry, Gill Ferris, Jo Newell, and John and Ian, the two sons of Joan's brother, Colin. The very large attendance of villagers and others was a fitting tribute to a true Guarlfordian.

So was completed another chapter in the story of Guarlford.

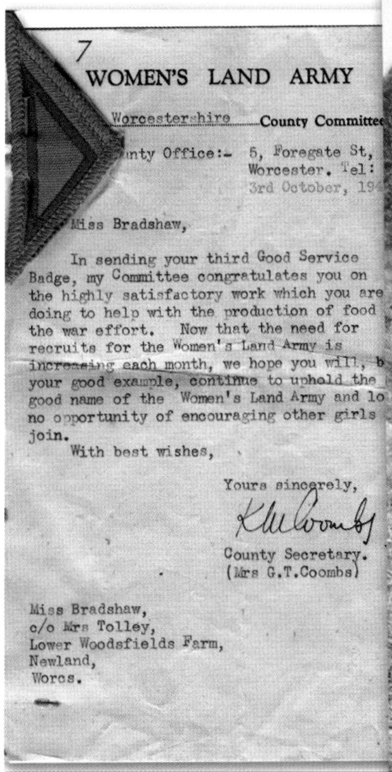

7

WOMEN'S LAND ARMY

Worcestershire County Committee

...nty Office:- 5, Foregate St,
Worcester. Tel:
3rd October, 194

Miss Bradshaw,

In sending your third Good Service Badge, my Committee congratulates you on the highly satisfactory work which you are doing to help with the production of food the war effort. Now that the need for recruits for the Women's Land Army is increasing each month, we hope you will, b your good example, continue to uphold the good name of the Women's Land Army and lo no opportunity of encouraging other girls join.

With best wishes,

Yours sincerely,

K M Coombs

County Secretary.
(Mrs G.T.Coombs)

Miss Bradshaw,
c/o Mrs Tolley,
Lower Woodsfields Farm,
Newland,
Worcs.

8

9

10

Figure 1.7 The Bradshaw Montage 2.

The Bradshaw Family Tree

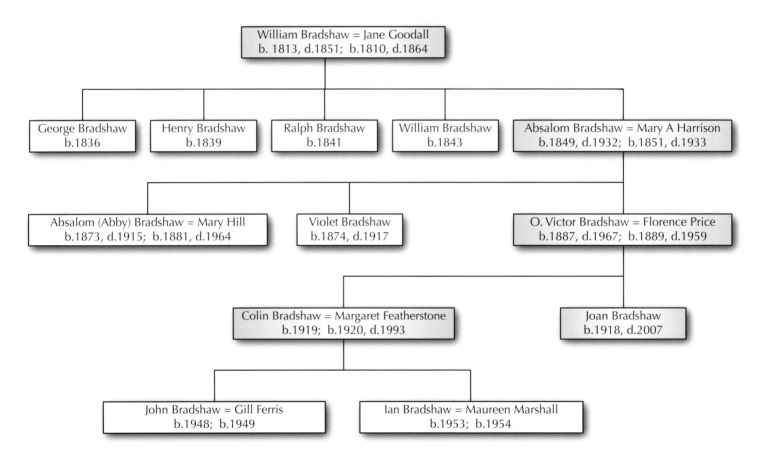

Figure 1.8 The Bradshaw Family Tree.

Figure 1.9 Joan Bradshaw's funeral at St Mary's Church, 10th May 2007.   (Michael Skinner).

The Gillett Burton Family

When farm labourers moved house in Guarlford before the Second World War, they would often borrow a horse and cart from their employer; but those people able to afford it could use the services of E Gillett Burton, who ran a removal business in the parish, as well as a taxi service, based at 'Laburnum House' on the Guarlford Road opposite the 'Green Dragon'. Behind the house was a warehouse for storing furniture, and Messrs Winwood, who took over the firm, also leased what is now the Village Hall for use as a furniture repository during the Second World War. Mr Burton's removal van can be seen (4) parked on the common outside 'Laburnum House' with Mr Burton on the left and in the middle Mr Archie Jones, who was also the driver of the taxi (6). Mr Burton is seen (1) on his wedding day, and then (2) in old age.

Other photographs, (3, 5 and 7) show a letter written by Mr Burton on the 4th August, 1934, to his employee, Mr Archie Jones. Note the address for telegrams "Burton, Guarlford, Malvern", and the telephone number "645" and how relatively simple these now appear – this was communication in a different age. The thoughtful, considerate letter reads:

Dear Jones,

I very much regret having to give you notice that your employment in my service as Furniture Remover will terminate as from 14 days next Monday, that is August 20. 1934. I again say how sorry I am to have to take this step, but I cannot do otherwise. I thank you very much for all you have done for me in the past & shall be very pleased to give you a really good reference if you apply to me at any time. The facts are these, much to my surprise about a fortnight ago I was offered, & have accepted, a directorship in Messrs Wm Winwoods of Worcester. They are taking over all my vans, stock-in-trade etc. The business in Malvern will be conducted by me as usual & will go on (exactly) as before, but as Messrs. Winwoods have 5 permanent men on their staff, not including myself, we do not as you can imagine require more & they will be used here in the Malvern business & so keep down expenses. I should strongly advise you to try your utmost at once to get another permanent job & anything I can do in the matter I will be only too pleased to do. I am writing to you as these matters are more easily expressed on paper & you can show the letter to your parents.
Yours sincerely,

E. Gillett Burton

Archie was then employed by Ally & McClelland, Worcester. He married Mary Nash in 1938; during the Second World War he worked on the famous 'Spitfires' and finished his working life at RRE Malvern, where he earned a long service medal.

E. GILLETT BURTON
Furniture Remover
GUARLFORD, MALVERN
Telegrams: BURTON, GUARLFORD, MALVERN.
Tel. 645

Aug 4. 34

Dear Jones.

I very much regret having to give you notice that your employment in my service as Furniture Remover, will terminate as from 14 days next Monday, that is August 20. 1934.

I again say how sorry I am to have to take this step, but I cannot do otherwise. I thank you very much for all you have done for me in the past & shall be very pleased to give you a really good reference if you apply to me at any time.

The facts are these, much to my surprise about a fortnight ago I was offered, & have yesterday accepted a Directorship in Messrs Wm Winwoods of Worcester.

They are taking over all my Vans stock in trade &c.

The business in Malvern will be conducted by me as usual & will go on (exactly) as before, but as Messrs Winwoods have 5 permanent men on their staff, not including myself, we do not [illegible] can imagine require more,

Removals of every description
Warehousing
PERSONAL SUPERVISION
E. GILLETT BURTON
Furniture Remover
GUARLFORD, MALVERN
Telegrams: BURTON, GUARLFORD, MALVERN.
Tel. 645

2

& they will be used here in the Malvern business to keep down expenses.

I should strongly advise you to try your utmost at once to get another permanent job & anything I can do in the matter I will be only too pleased to do. I am writing to you as these matters are more easily expressed on paper & you can show the letter to your parent.

Yours sincerely E Gillett Burton

Figure 1.10 The Gillett Burton Montage.

The Hayes and Clarke Families

The Hayes and the Clarke families are long-established in Guarlford and appear often in the story of the parish. During the First World War, the Clarke family lived in one of the New House Farm cottages. Fred is seen (1) wearing uniform and beside him is his wife, Lily. The two small boys are Harold, father of Mrs Doreen Williams, and Bernard, father of Mrs Daphne Hayes. Fred was the cowman for the Medcalfs; later Bernard also milked the cows and cared for the pigs, while Harold became the wagoner's boy and eventually the tractor driver at New House Farm.

Mr Harry Hayes came from the Birmingham area to 122 Clevelode at the end of the nineteenth century and brought with him the art of weaving baskets from osiers. His son, Thomas, worked firstly as a male nurse at the Powick Asylum and then as a basket-maker. He lived at Rhydd and later at Hilltop Cottage, Clevelode, where he specialised in fine work.

The Great War involved every family in the village in some way, and Thomas Hayes, wearing the uniform of the Worcestershire Regiment (2), was enlisted in May 1917, just before his thirty-eighth birthday. The family then had to survive on Thomas's army pay of 1/6d, as shown in his Pay Book. After training at Devonport, he was sent straight to France, but in July 1918 was reported missing. Until the Red Cross managed to discover that Thomas was alive, his wife Edith had to fear the worst. He was, in fact, a prisoner of war and was repatriated in January 1919.

Thomas's son, Roland, is with his wife (3). Roland, father of Clifford, spent all his life as a basket-maker beside the river at Clevelode and could turn his hand to making almost anything from osiers. The life of a basket-maker was hard, and Mr Hayes often used to work twelve hours a day, his hands covered with calluses from bending the withies to the desired shape.

A family party was held when Bernard Clarke, one of the small boys of the First World War, celebrated his ninetieth birthday in 2002 (4). Bernard and his wife, Nina, lived in a cottage at the crossroads near St Mary's Church, and their daughter, Daphne, married Clifford Hayes in 1964. The photograph shows four generations: Mrs Nina Clarke, with her daughter, Daphne Hayes, and grand-daughter, Becky Hayes; Bernard Clarke is with his great-grandson, Daniel Humphrey, and grand-daughter, Judith Humphrey (nee Hayes), and his son, David Clarke.

Figure 1.11 The Hayes Montage.

The Lane Family

Members of the Lane family have lived at Woodbridge Farm since at least 1762, when a John Lane is recorded as the tenant. The family has therefore been involved in the life of the village for nearly 250 years. By 1775, the family had purchased the property, then a smallholding of about seven acres, and over the years the family acquired more land. Edwin Lane, the present owner, himself farmed the land until 2000, when he retired and sold most of the acreage, retaining just the house and the adjoining two small fields that comprised the original smallholding. John Lane's grandson, George Lane (1796 – 1882), is to be seen in this very early photograph (1). The name of George's father appears on the first page of the Church Burials Register for the new St Mary's Church, when he was buried in the churchyard on 1st April, 1846.

Young Sarah Andrews (1824 – 1895), a schoolteacher from Bushley (2), and George's son, Edwin (1827 - 1887) in (3) were married on the 5th November, 1850, while (4) is a later picture of Edwin and Sarah Lane.

The elegant wedding (5) is of their grandson, Arthur Edwin Lane (born in 1895) to Alice Smith at St John's Church, Brockmore, Brierley Hill, in October, 1930. In the back row are: Miss Olwen Lane (bridegroom's sister), Mr William Smith (bride's father), and Cyril James Lane and Harold Thomas Lane (bridegroom's brothers). In the front row: May Noble, Alice Smith (bride), Arthur Edwin Lane

(bridegroom) and Margaret Louisa George. Arthur and Alice were the parents of the present owner, Edwin Lane, and his sister, Mrs Margaret Omar. Edwin and Margaret have many memories of their childhood in Guarlford. They recall the haymaking at Woodbridge Farm; their job as children was to take baskets with cider and sandwiches to the haymakers. Beside the wagon around 1936 (6) are visitors, Mr William Smith (brother of Edwin's mother), his wife, Emily, and their children, Mary and John, with a little Margaret Lane (now Omar) and Edwin – together with, of course, Edwin's dog, 'Rinty', named after 'Rin Tin Tin'.

As children, Edwin and Margaret lived just along the lane from Woodbridge Farm at 'The Bungalow', now 'Jasmine Cottage'. Around 1941, Mr Arthur Lane is with Edwin and Margaret (7), who clearly recall the Radio Hut, the masts and network of aerials being erected in the field beside their home. An army lorry with an aerial on the roof had earlier parked near the field on various occasions, obviously seeking the best radio reception, and finally the Hut was built – and it was reported that people walking past could hear strange bleeps!

Figure 1.12 The Lane Montage.

The Lane Family Tree

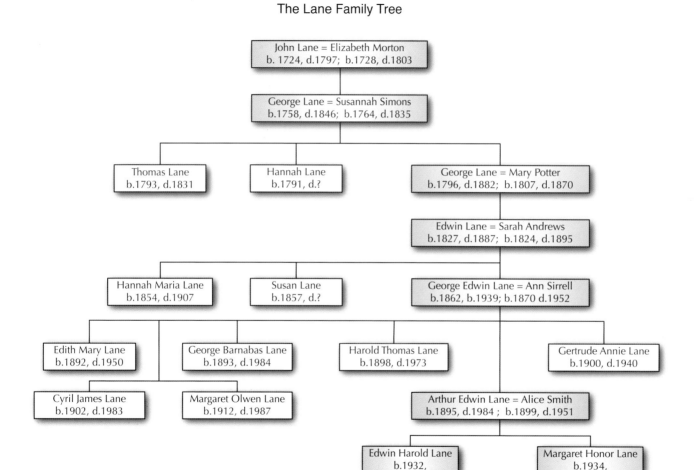

Figure 1.13 The Lane Family Tree.

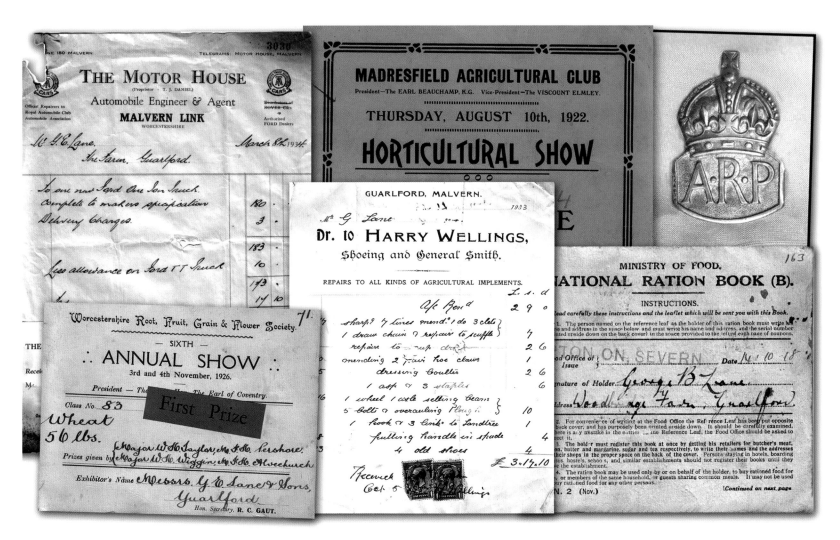

Figure 1.14 Lane Family Memorabilia.

The Little Family, c.1906

Standing
George; Herbert and John (Jack).

Seated
Annie; Frank; Mother Mary Ann with baby Leonard; Arthur; Father John with toddler James (Jim);
and
Alice, the eldest daughter, at the front.

This photograph was taken in 1906 at 'Severnside', by the River Severn at Clevelode, where Mr John Little plied his trade as a salmon fisherman, as recorded on the 1901 Census.

Except for Herbert, who, sadly, was killed in the First World War, on August 22nd 1917, the children grew up into a fine family, as can be seen in the photograph from 1950 which is reproduced on page 58 of *The Guarlford Story*.

Fig 1.15 The Little Family at Severnside, Clevelode, c.1906.

The Little Family

The Little family are to be seen in 1910 (5), when they had won the prize at the Madresfield Show for the largest family living on the Madresfield Estate. In the back row are George, born in 1890, John, b.1892, and Herbert, b. 1894; in the front row are Frank, b. 1901, Annie, b. 1897, and their mother, Mary Little, holding baby Walter, b. 1909, followed by James, born in 1903, their father John Little with Leonard, b. 1905, on his knee, Alice, b. 1896, with Emmie, b. 1908, and Arthur, b. 1899. Two more children were born to the family – Sidney and Jessie.

Having a large family means there are many links with other Guarlford families, and events like weddings were very well attended. The large group (3) shows the close family of the bride, Hilda Sims, and groom, Arthur Little. The wedding took place in Guarlford in 1926, and the reception was held at 'Southwood', Clevelode, home of the bride's parents. Her father, George (known as 'Jarvey') Sims, was a woodsman. Of the thirty people in the photograph, twenty-six are named – Littles, Sims, Clarkes, Pritchards and Owens, all from well-known Guarlford families. The bride and groom are flanked by the groom's brother, Jack Little, and bride's brother, Bill Sims. The two seated bridesmaids are (left) Emmie Little (groom's sister) and (right) Rose Sims, (bride's sister). Arthur's mother, Mary, is seated next to Emmie, and Hilda's parents, George ('Jarvey') and Rose Hannah Sims, are next to the other bridesmaid, Rose.

Living right beside the River Severn at Clevelode, the members of the Little family naturally found employment in fishing, particularly for salmon and eels. Three of the brothers, Sidney, Len and Walter, are sorting out their fishing net (2). Salmon were caught in a large net made of hemp with a six inch mesh, which allowed small salmon and other fish to escape; there were four inch cubes of cork along one side and lead weights along the other. The net would be held against one bank, while the fishermen used a flat-bottomed punt with paddles to pull it across the river, as Len Little is doing (4). By then, working in a circular movement, they caught any salmon swimming upstream. Chapter 4 of *The Guarlford Story* has accounts of salmon fishing and eel catching at Clevelode.

Figure 1.16 The Little Montage.

The Medcalf Family

Since 1884, when Stephen George Medcalf (1) took on the tenancy of New House Farm, members of the family have been involved continuously in Guarlford village life. Mr Stephen Medcalf was born in Sussex in 1862 and, after working on a farm in Berkshire, came to the Court Farm in 1883, before moving to New House Farm, which he later bought from the Foley Estate in the great sale of 1910. He was one of the first people elected as a Guarlford Parish Councillor in 1894, a position later held in their turn by his son Derrick, his grandson, Bill, and his great-grandson, Andrew, who is a Councillor at present. He was also a Church Warden, District Councillor, a Guardian, and an Overseer, whose task was to collect from parishioners the money needed for Parish Relief and then distribute it to the poor.

Stephen, who died in 1926, married Sarah Maria, pictured (7) with their sons, Derrick, and Stephen John, known as 'Jack'. When Jack (born 1893) wanted to continue growing hops (discontinued at New House Farm in the 1920s), he rented Cliffey Farm at Rhydd from the Lechmeres' Severn End Estate, later moving to Cotheridge. Derrick (1896 – 1972) and his wife, Ethel, are still remembered in Guarlford today, as they were so much part of the working and social life of the neighbourhood. Mrs Ethel Medcalf (2) was a founder member of Guarlford W I in 1941, and later President. She died in 1977, aged 79, and her obituary in the June Parish Magazine describes "... the spare and active figure no longer with us... who was so generous in time and hospitality".

Derrick's son, Bill, photographed with his wife Edna (3), continued, like his forebears, to work hard on the farm and in the village community until his death in 1998. One of the village's Millennium commemorative trees, a black poplar, was planted in memory of Bill on the Guarlford Road common near the farm.

Horse-riding was one of Bill's favourite pastimes, a love inherited by his descendants, including two of his grand-daughters shown here, (5) Sarah Medcalf, who enjoys triathlon competitions, and (6) Rosie Fellowes, daughter of David and Sue (nee Medcalf). Sarah's father, Andrew, pictured (4) with his wife, Linda, and son, Stephen, in 1991, continues to farm New House Farm.

Figure 1.17 The Medcalf Montage.

The Newson Family

In 1920 the beautiful eighteen year old Frances May Jackson of Priestfields (1) married the eligible Reverend Frederick John Newson (pictured in (3) in his uniform as Chaplain to the Forces during the First World War). So began a marriage that was a blessing for Guarlford. For the next forty five years the couple made Guarlford Rectory a welcoming centre for the village and a happy home for their family. (2) Shows the Newson family in about 1950: Betty, Mrs Newson and the Revd Newson with, in front, Richard, Pamela, Guy (son of Betty) and Michael. The photograph was taken beside the mulberry tree in the Rectory garden, which despite being blown over onto its side still bears fruit.

Revd Newson was Rector of Guarlford from 1913 until 1964. He was a great support to his parishioners, and (4) shows him as many remember him today. Throughout her husband's ministry, Mrs Newson supported church and parish activities – fetes, dancing classes, Poppy Day collections, Sunday School and its outings, tennis parties for young people – and in the Second World War the family welcomed many evacuees to the Rectory. Daughter Betty had an amazing escape in 1941. At 1 am on 29th April, about 700 miles west of Fastnet, the 'City of Nagpur', on which she was travelling to South Africa to join her first husband, was torpedoed and sunk by the German submarine U-75. Kapitanleutnant Ringelmann gave them time to evacuate the ship, and the majority of passengers and crew were able to take to the lifeboats.

They were later spotted by the pilot of a 'Catalina' flying boat, who telegraphed 'HMS Hurricane' to come to their aid. The full story of this great adventure can be seen on the GHG Memories page of the parish website: www.guarlford.org.uk.

In 1941, Mrs Newson helped to found Guarlford WI, whose ladies met weekly to make jam, knit socks and blankets and even make camouflage nets. At the same time, she joined the St John Ambulance, initially to help with First Aid but eventually becoming Superintendent of the Malvern Division, even acting as driver for Lady Louis Mountbatten, Superintendent-in-Chief, on her wartime visit to Worcestershire. In 1980, Mrs Newson was made a Commander of St John at the Grand Priory Lodge in the City of London (7), and (5) shows her in 1986 holding the cake celebrating the 70th anniversary of the Malvern Nursing Division of the St John Ambulance.

After the War, Mrs Newson started the Crèche at the Three Counties Show for which she received an award presented by Princess Alexandra. (6) Shows Mrs Newson with some of her young charges. When the Revd F Newson retired after more than 50 years incumbency, they moved to the Beauchamp Community at Newland, and for thirty years Mrs Newson gave her energies to the community there.

Figure 1.18 The Newson Montage.

The Panting Family 1

The Panting family featured prominently in the story of Guarlford when Mrs Myra Panting (1) lost both her grandsons in the First World War, after her husband had died in 1915 and her son in 1917. Mrs Panting is shown knitting one of over one hundred pairs of socks she made during the war, in spite of failing sight. Her grandson, Thomas, died of his wounds in 1917, and his brother, Philip, was killed in action just a month after arriving in France in 1918. The montage (Figure 1.21) shows the military funeral of Thomas in Guarlford Churchyard. The *Malvern News* reported "The Military Authorities at Woolwich made themselves responsible for the conveyance of the body to Malvern, where by the kindness of the Wireless Depot (a Royal Engineers training depot at Worcester), a military funeral was arranged." The Revd F Newson officiated at the service, which included a military salute of three rifle volleys and the sounding of the Last Post.

William and Myra Panting lived in a small cottage in Clevelode Lane, as seen in 1909 (2). In his memoirs, their grandson, Reg Green, described how his grandfather, "a farm worker all his life", was crippled by gout for many years. In old age, the couple survived on 'parish pay'.

Ellen Thornbury Panting, who was born in 1866, lived until 1950, and is still remembered in the village today (4). Ellen was married to William and Myra's son, Thomas, and had the great sadness of losing not only her husband at the age of sixty-one, but also her sons, Thomas and Philip, as well as her beautiful daughter, Myra (5), born in 1900 and pictured as a baby with her mother in (3). Myra died aged 23 years, a few months after she had married Jack Reed.

Ellen's third son, Joseph, born in 1901, lived until 1973. Joseph was photographed (7) with his wife Lily (nee Edwards) sometime in the 1920s. He served with the Warwickshire Regiment after the First World War. He is near the Khyber Pass (8), accompanied by a pet monkey. Joseph was at Dunkirk early in the Second World War.

When Lily was a child, her parents were employed at Croome Court, the home of the Earls of Coventry, and (6) shows her in what is possibly her confirmation dress in about 1915. She worked at Callow End before her marriage to Joseph, and the couple had three daughters.

The eldest daughter, Dorothy, born in 1923, remembers leading Shire horses for her father when he worked for Mr Wall at Madresfield and "picking up stones" in the fields on Whittakers Farm (Whiteacres) with her mother to prepare the ground for the harrow. Hard work and painful hands were eased by the pleasure of watching plovers and curlews swooping over the pond.

Figure 1.19 The Panting Montage 1.

The Panting Family Tree

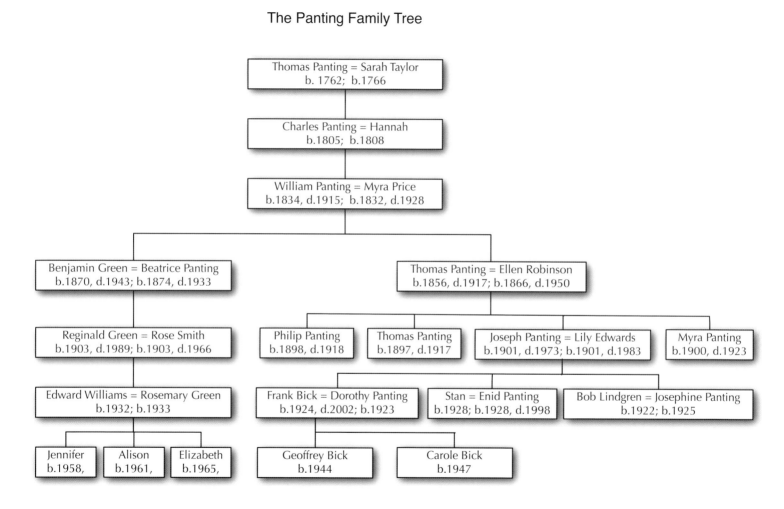

Figure 1.20 The Panting Family Tree.

Philip Panting

Funeral of Thomas Panting RA, 19th May 1917

Thomas Panting

Figure 1.21 The Funeral of Thomas Panting, 19th May 1917.

The Panting Family 2

In the Second World War, the women of the Panting family were also 'called up'. In about 1940, Dorothy, aged seventeen, wears her WRNS uniform (9); she was based at 'HMS Ganges', near Ipswich, as Captain's messenger, and then moved to London to work in the Pay Office. On January 24, 1944, when both had a week's leave, Dorothy married Able Seaman Frank Ernest Bick of Rhydd: Frank is pictured on September 7, 1942 (11). Dorothy and Frank had attended Guarlford School together. Frank joined the Royal Navy as a boy sailor, and in the Second World War was based in Portsmouth, serving on 'HMS Nelson' and 'HMS Belfast'; the latter is now moored on the River Thames. Dorothy remembers cycling to the Malvern Registry Office to organise the licence and how, on their wedding day, they were on their way to Malvern when Dorothy's hat was blown off on to the railway line – Frank gallantly climbed down to fetch it. Their wedding cake was a mince pie! Frank died on 19th December, 2002, just over a year before they would have celebrated their sixtieth wedding anniversary.

Dorothy's sister, Josephine Lilian Panting, here seen on December 31, 1945 (14), worked at TRE in the Second World War, married a scientist, and moved to the USA. Now Mrs Robert Lindgren, she lives there still.

The photograph of the youngest sister, Enid Barbara Panting, born in 1928, is dated 16th December, 1944 (13). She served in the Land Army for a while and married Stan Rone of Madresfield. Enid died in 2001.

These three beautiful women, so perfectly photographed, are worthy grand-daughters of Ellen, who stands in the garden of 'The Orchard', Clevelode (10).

Reg Green (12) was the son of Ellen's sister-in-law, Beatrice Panting, who married Benjamin Green and settled in Dudley, and is the father of Rosemary Williams who, with her husband the Reverend Edward Williams, now lives in Penny Lane. Reg's memoirs paint vivid pictures of Guarlford in the first half of the twentieth century. When Reg could not find work in Dudley, he "got on his bike", literally, and cycled to Guarlford to stay with his grandmother, Myra. He then worked at New House Farm for twenty-five years. Reg's memoir, written for his family, is aptly entitled *I Got on My Bike*, and provided a valuable source for *The Guarlford Story*. Reg became a Town Councillor and is proudly wearing the chain of office of the Chairman of Malvern Urban District Council, a position he held 1967-68.

Figure 1.22 The Panting Montage 2.

The Shinn Family

When the name of Arthur Shinn is mentioned, people who lived in the area from the 1930s onwards always remember his bees and the wonderful honey produced at the pretty black and white cottage on the Guarlford Road. Mr Arthur Shinn, as can be seen, won many prizes and awards for his honey at local and county shows (1).

Members of the Shinn family have lived at their cottage (3) for over a hundred years. William Shinn, Arthur's father, is recorded in the 1901 Census as a twenty-six year old post office clerk, lodging with the tenant of 170 Guarlford Road, Mrs Hannah Woodland, aged sixty-three. William married her daughter, Annie Woodland, who was also twenty-six, soon after. In the 1910 Foley Estate Sale William bought the cottage, here seen with its thatched roof from across the common. Note the pollarded black poplar still standing at the gateway and Mr Medcalf's hopfields to the right.

William and Annie had three children. In the family group (4) from about 1925 are from left to right: William Henry Shinn, daughter, Hilda Muriel, wife, Annie Louisa, and their two sons, Arthur Cecil and Percy Leslie. Percy moved to 'Blackmore' at Hanley Swan when he married, and Arthur and his family shared the Guarlford Road cottage with Hilda. Miss Hilda Shinn was well-known in the parish; she was born in 1912 and lived in the cottage until her death in 2000.

Arthur was a keen sportsman, both in village teams - especially the Football Club, as can be seen in the account of the Guarlford Football Club - and at school. He attended the Lyttelton Grammar School, which was a small school, now the Lyttelton Rooms, built in the grounds of Great Malvern Priory. Robert Bartleet's father was Vicar of the Priory from 1919 to 1946 and governor as well as Chaplain of the school until its closure. Arthur is third from the left in the back row in the very traditional, slightly austere school photograph (2). He later moved to Hanley Castle Grammar School.

The Lyttelton Grammar School was founded in 1874 to provide boys for the Priory choir. Evidently, the school used the old Sunday School rooms, which had been built by Lady Lyttelton in 1817, and then rebuilt in 1886. One source describes the era of Mr Thornton as Headmaster of the Lyttelton Grammar School from 1903 until 1933, together with the appointment of Dr Louis Hamand, as choirmaster in 1910, as "... one of the high points of music at the Priory, with daily rehearsals for the boys to prepare for the Cathedral-style repertoire". Sadly, by 1946, financial difficulties forced the closure of Lyttelton School. The nearest grammar schools were then in Worcester and Hanley Castle.

Figure 1.23 The Shinn Montage.

The Smith Family

Mr Ron Smith came to Guarlford in 1939, when he took on the tenancy of Guarlford Court Farm, a huge challenge for him. Ron was determined to farm on his own, especially as he had just become engaged to Dorrie, whose father had forbidden them to marry until he was in a position to provide for her, and (1) was taken when Ronald Herman Smith and Doris Mary Smith were married two years later in 1941 at St John's Church, Hagley. (Dorrie's maiden name was also Smith.) The couple worked very hard on the farm, having to take into their home evacuees from Bournville, as well as coping with other aspects of wartime living. Dorrie recalled that at least food shortages were not so bad for them, as they had their own milk, eggs, fruit, vegetables and poultry, and sometimes a pig.

The couple had two daughters, Meriel and Alison; (2) shows the family in 1956 at their home, Guarlford Court, and (7), Meriel and Alison with the milk churns awaiting collection, was taken in 1958. The family has always been very involved in village life, with Meriel following her father as a Churchwarden.

Alison married Peter Watkins on 22nd August 1990, and (6) shows them outside St Mary's Church, Guarlford. In the picture are (left to right): Trevor Bethell (the best man), Mrs. Dorrie Smith, Alison and Peter Watkins, Meriel Smith and Mr Ron Smith, with small bridesmaids Freda and Patricia Davis.

Ron and Dorrie Smith celebrated their own Golden Wedding anniversary on 4th June, 1991. They are seen (3) cutting their cake at a surprise party in Faith Cottage, the home of Miss Helen Smith (Dorrie's sister), who had arranged the party with Meriel. Miss Helen Smith devoted much of her time to St Mary's Church, helping in many ways, including looking after the altar and playing the organ, as in (5), in the late 1980s at the wedding of Mike and Shelagh Thorne.

On 7th December, 2002, Meriel married Francis Bennett in St Mary's, Guarlford, and the service was attended by many people from the village, who wanted to wish this popular couple well. Francis and Meriel are seen (4) after the service – Meriel is wearing a particularly attractive dress, made in a medieval style.

Mr Ron Smith died in 1997 and Mrs Dorrie Smith in 2003. Dorrie celebrated her 90th birthday on Millennium Eve, and festivities included the party in the Village Hall.

Figure 1.24 The Smith Montage.

The Vivian Family

Members of the Vivian family are seen in 1908 (2) outside their black and white cottage in Blakes Lane, Guarlford. Standing beside the front door is Mrs Florence May Vivian with William Henry Jnr, and in front of them are Roderick Victor, Lilian Ruby and Florence Emily, who is holding the baby. The Vivians moved into the cottage in 1900 as tenants of the Madresfield Estate and later purchased it in the sale of 1919. William Henry Snr worked locally as a carrier with his own horse and cart. He was, however, a bricklayer by trade, and it is believed that he built the stone wall around the churchyard.

Roderick Victor Vivian, born 1901, is pictured (1) with his wife Rachel (nee Reynolds). They met when both were employed at 'Kents Green Court'. Rachel had come from Carmarthen to work as a maid, and Roderick worked on the farm, caring especially for the horses, for which he was particularly recommended by his employer, Mrs Winsmore Hooper. By 1935, Rod was working for Mr Bladder at Fowler's Farm, Guarlford, and *The Guarlford Story* p.21 describes him as the groom for the Shire stallions at stud, taking 'Dripshill Forest King' round the county to various farms. He later became cowman at Dripshill Farm.

Rachel, Rod's wife, is at the cottage gate (3) with Roderick William Thomas Vivian, who was born in 1925. This Roderick was always known as 'Bill'. Rachel was one of the founder members of Guarlford W I. Roderick Vivian Snr joined the Guarlford Football Club as Secretary in the late 1920s. He served on the committee in several capacities for many years, as did his sons, Victor and Bill, and the Blakes Lane cottage was the venue for many committee meetings.

Rod died in 1977, and his obituary in the Guarlford Parish magazine, described him as a "... fine villager... steady character and fine professional gardener." He had worked for a while at the Blackmore Army Camp, and then at the 'Montrose Hotel' in Graham Road, Great Malvern. Here Rod not only looked after the grounds but also grew vegetables for the hotel kitchen, as well as flowers for the rooms. He was also well known at the Madresfield Show, where he won many prizes for his flowers and vegetables.

Rod's grandson, Tom, and his family now live in the cottage in Blakes Lane, which he re-developed in 1997. Tom and his wife, Jill, are developing the garden, and the colourful dahlias, always a feature of the garden in Rod's day, are being re-introduced.

Figure 1.25 The Vivian Montage.

The Whitlock Family

Mr Thomas Whitlock was born in Wilton Road, Malvern, and came to live in 'Foley Cottage', Chance Lane, in 1932, when he married Eva, nee Goodyear, who was born in 'Archer's Cottage', Sherrard's Green. Eva was photographed in about 1926 (3). Thomas and Eva were courting for ten years before they married, as Tom was saving to buy 'Foley Cottage' for themselves and also to purchase the house in Wilton Road for his mother.

Tom served in the Fire Brigade and was an Officer in Charge of the Upton-upon-Severn Section. He volunteered to serve in the London 'Blitz' in the Second World War. Tom is second left in a scene of destruction with particularly smartly-uniformed officers standing amidst the rubble (1), and also in the pre-1939 photograph of Malvern Fire Brigade (7).

Tom volunteered for army service and is in the uniform of the Royal Army Service Corps (2). He was a driver, and he brought back to England a fabric road map of the Dunkirk area, which has a water stain across it made when he stood waist high in the sea waiting for rescue. Tom was finally evacuated from the beaches near Dunkirk, as described in the diary he kept at the time:

"No idea of time or day or date. Long march. Dusty French & Belgian soldiers, Cavalry, Coloured Infantry & Artillery, thousands travelling in all directions. Started to march over sand dunes, rifles keep clogging with sand in the breeze. Belgian or French Cavalry still with us. They seem to be making for the same place. No-one hardly speaks, just keeps marching. Arrive at Braydunes. Warships in bay, one paddle-boat bombed and burning, looks like one of Campbell's, Cardiff. One other bombed and burning, bad in bay, two others just been sunk. 10 pm Ralf Buckle swims and gets boat, taken on trawler Ocean Breeze. Bombed and machine gunned, get away. Ta-ta Braydunes. Attacked by plane out at sea. Arrived Ramsgate 5.30 am next morning."

Tom's son, John (4), is in his National Service RAF uniform. John served from 1955 to 1958, finally becoming personal steward to the AOC 27 Group, RAF Cherill, near Calne, Wiltshire.

Judy Whitlock, aged 18, is at 'Foley Cottage' (5). In about 1951, Richard Young, of the 'Smithy' at Hall Green, Orlean Mary Young, nee Whitlock, and John Whitlock are pictured together (6). Orlean recalls that, as a teenager after the War, she had to put on make-up by candlelight, because, although electricity had come to the 'Green Dragon' area of the Guarlford Road before the Second World War, there was none in Chance Lane until 1955.

The Whitlocks lived in 'Foley Cottage' until 1979.

Figure 1.26 The Whitlock Montage.

The Williams Family

Charlie Williams is a familiar figure in the area who has, with his phenomenal memory, a fund of tales of the local countryside. He was born in Twyning in 1923, and the Williams family came to live in Hanley Castle when Charlie was three years old. As a boy, Charlie listened to many stories about rural life and also the Great War. Charlie's brother, Tom, who spent his seventeenth birthday on a First World War battlefield in France, also 'Answered His Country's Call' (1) in the Second World War, when he volunteered and served as a sergeant on an anti-aircraft gun in Swindon.

During the Second World War, Charlie worked for Mr Ron Smith at Guarlford Court, and this was when he earned the British Empire Medal clearly seen on his lapel (3). Charlie, here with his parents and his sister, Alice, was very strong, which was lucky for the Australian pilot, Bob Morris. The story of Charlie's very brave rescue of Bob on 22nd April, 1944, from a burning 'Beaufighter' aircraft which crashed near Southwood is recounted in *The Guarlford Story*, pp.152 and 153. Bob Morris was unconscious for a fortnight and in hospital for nine months. Charlie received his medal from King George VI at Buckingham Palace. Eventually, Bob recovered and returned to Australia, from where he sent a congratulatory cable on the occasion of Charlie's twenty-first birthday in December 1944. Bob died in 2002, and his son, Stanley, came to Britain from Australia in 2003 and presented Charlie with the wallet his father had been carrying in the crash, together with a photograph of the Morris family, who owed Charlie so much. Charlie and Stanley stand beside the very crab-apple tree near which the plane crashed (4).

Horses have always played an important part in Charlie's life. He says, "As soon as I could scrobble, all I thought about was the horses." Charlie was the last person in Guarlford to cut corn with horses and the last to plough with them. He remembers that the young men returning after the Second World War preferred the new 'Fergie' tractors to horses, and so the faithful, hard-working animals became redundant.

It was only to be expected perhaps that after Charlie's wedding to Doreen Clarke, of New House Farm cottages, in March, 1958, in St Mary's Church, Guarlford, the happy couple would travel from the church on a carriage labelled 'Dun Roamin' drawn by 'Bluebell' (2).

Charlie has passed this love of horses on to his children, and daughter, Jackie, is with 'Lacetown Quicksilver' at 'The Three Villages Rideabout' in 1986 (5).

Figure 1.27 The Williams Montage.

Chapter 2

Guarlford's Buildings

Introduction

Village buildings themselves provide a record of the history of a place, and most English villages have certain types of buildings in common. The church, farm buildings and small cottages, in particular, help to delineate the boundaries as well as the evolution of the original settlements that became established villages. Its proximity to Malvern and common land perhaps meant that Guarlford never acquired the village green or centre that characterize the "typical" English village; but from the 1840s onwards, with the building of the church, Guarlford combined continuity and change in much the same way as other villages. The school, the several shops of the village and the blacksmiths served the modestly thriving village population and were focal points on the landscape. Guarlford Parish, including the hamlets of Clevelode and Rhydd, still has a wide variety of buildings, which illustrate and reflect the many facets of village life over the centuries.

Guarlford Court is the village's main substantial link back to the Medieval past. Other, less old, buildings, such as New House Farm and Cherry Orchard, were extended and made larger in one or two phases as the owners prospered in later centuries. Sadly, many much smaller homes have been demolished, like the cottages in the parish occupied by agricultural workers, which were no longer needed as farming became less labour-intensive. Many of these stood along the 'Guarlford Straight' or in the fields nearby. In recent times, two traditional cottages at the end of Rectory Lane opposite the church were replaced by bungalows. 'Maywood', on the other hand, the cottage in which Marie Hall once lived, survives enlarged and extended.

The use of other Guarlford buildings has changed over the years. Some farmhouses, such as Guarlford Court and Cherry Orchard, have become private dwellings, while barns have also been converted into homes. Similarly, part of the Malt House, which served the whole village between 1870 and 1911, when it was surrounded by Cherry Orchard Farm, subsequently became the village Men's Club and, later, the Village Hall of today.

Dusty Work by Tom Vivian.

Houses Changing With the Times

Guarlford Court

Some of the parish's most prominent houses were at one time farmhouses. As farms have been amalgamated, these former farmhouses, no longer the hub of family farm life, have been let out or sold. One of these is Guarlford Court (2.1) on the opposite page. Guarlford Court is probably Guarlford's oldest dwelling, with its origins in the thirteenth century, when it was a demesne farm, part of the Malvern Priory Estate. Members of the Worcestershire Historical Society visited the Court before the Second World War, and found that the beams in the kitchen were over 600 years old.

Soon after the dissolution of the monasteries in the sixteenth century, the Guarlford Court Farm was sold by the Crown, and passed through the hands of several families until it was purchased by the Berkeleys of Spetchley in the seventeenth century. By the end of the nineteenth century, it was owned by the Madresfield Estate; and, in 1898, the late Miss Joan Bradshaw's grandfather, Absalom Bradshaw, became the tenant farmer. His son, Victor, took the tenancy after Absalom's retirement, and Joan and her brother grew up at the Court. The picture (2.2), though rather obviously posed, captures a sunny moment towards the end of the nineteenth century when the pony, as well as Mr and Mrs Absalom Bradshaw, appears very conscious of the photographer's presence.

The view of the Court, c.1900, shows the pond in front of the extensive building, and members of the Bradshaw family can be seen in the garden. The eighteenth century dovecote is visible on the right of the main house.

In 1939, Mr Ron Smith took the tenancy of Guarlford Court for an annual rent of £1 per acre. Although he and his wife, Dorrie, lived at the Court at first, from 1966 they let the house out and lived in a nearby cottage. In 1983, when Ron retired, the Madresfield Estate sold the house to today's residents, Toby and Margaretha Bruce-Morgan.

Figure 2.1 (Above) Guarlford Court c.1900.

Figure 2.2 (Above right) Joan Bradshaw's grandparents, Mr and Mrs Absalom Bradshaw in 'The Tub' pulled by Tommy the pony, around 1898.

Figure 2.3 (Right) Guarlford Court 2007.   (Peter Mayner).

This is the same view of the Court as in Figure 2.2, taken in 2007.

Cherry Orchard

Figure 2.4 Cherry Orchard, c.1900.

Figure 2.5 Cherry Orchard, 2007. *(Peter Mayner).*

Cherry Orchard around 1900 (opposite page), another former farmhouse, appears with the Robathan family posing beneath the veranda, Mother, father and three sons, with grandmother in the window. The veranda is covered by a canvas canopy and the upper windows also have folding sunshades. The stone wall of the 'ha ha' is visible between the garden and field. A 'ha ha' is a field boundary to keep stock in, formed by a deep ditch with perpendic-ular wall on one side, from the bottom of the ditch to ground level, which therefore does not obstruct a view. Cherry Orchard, now the home of Dr and Mrs Peter Mayner, has not changed significantly in outward appearance. A conservatory, though, now stands alongside the house on the right. This has been the venue for many meetings of the authors of the two Guarlford history books.

New House Farm

Figure 2.6 New House Farm, c.1905.

The photograph above shows the original Georgian farmhouse, built in the 1700s, with hop kilns on the left, and the pond in front of the garden wall. The Victorian-style addition to the front of the house in about 1908 is seen (2.7); this is one of several farmhouses in the parish which were extended and remodelled as the owners prospered. Compare the truncated hop kilns with those in the earlier photograph, and notice the initials, 'N H F' adorning the roof. The horseman is believed to be Jack Medcalf.

Figure 2.7 New House Farm, 2007. (*Janet Lomas*).

The Rectory

Figure 2.8 Children dancing in front of the Rectory at the Church Fete in 1911 when the incumbent was the Reverend Hubert Jones. The Rectory has remained largely unchanged to the present day, as may be seen from the insert.

Severnside, Clevelode

Figure 2.9 This photograph was taken in 1998, and shows Clare Roberts, daughter of Chris, at 'Severnside', which overlooks the river at Clevelode; the house has now been completely rebuilt, as shown in the insert.

Black and White Cottages

Bluebell Hall

A reproduction of a postcard picture (2.10), printed in the first half of the twentieth century, shows two semi-detached thatched cottages on the edge of the ecclesiastical parish at Mill Lane, now converted to one cottage and known as 'Bluebell Hall'. Between the wars, Alf Bosworth, who lived in the left hand cottage until the early 1950s, ran a plant nursery, and had several greenhouses. The other cottage housed 'Barber's General Store' which locals recall selling sweets, cigarettes and Carr's biscuits.

The background is of interest, with the bare hills or 'balg-dun' which gave their name to Baldenhall (house of the bare hills). The hills were at that time well grazed by livestock under the stewardship of the Malvern Hills Conservators.

The Malvern Hills Conservators also planted a beautiful avenue of trees down the Guarlford Road. The scar on the hills in the centre of the photograph is Earnslaw Quarry, which was still active at that time. The Malvern Hills Conservators were instrumental in closing the quarries. They then embarked on a programme of work to hide the scars with new growth including imported Alpine flora.

Figure 2.10 (Top left) Bosworth's Nursery and Barber's General Stores. The young trees visible here are a lime on the left hand side of the picture, an English oak in front of the cottage, and within the tree guards, Red oaks. The oaks are seen in their maturity in figure 2.12 taken in 2007.

Figure 2.11 (Top right) Mr Bosworth's Cottage.

Figure 2.12 (Bottom right) Bluebell Hall, 2007.   (Peter Mayner).

Figure 2.13 (Bottom left) Bluebell Hall, under restoration in 1999/2000.   (Howard Ashford).

170 Guarlford Road

Figure 2.14 Front view of 170 Guarlford Road, opposite the junction with Chance Lane, in the early years of the twentieth century.

Figure 2.15 (Left) Rear view of the cottage.

An old view of the back of 170 Guarlford Road, when the building was a thatched cottage, opposite the junction of Chance Lane with the 'Guarlford Straight'. William Shinn, grandfather of the present owner, Keith, bought the house from the Foley Estate in 1910.

Figure 2.16 (Right) Rent Receipt.

A receipt for 'Two half year's' rent due to Lady Emily Foley in 1855. The receipt is made out to Thomas Costin, Keith Shinn's great great grandfather.

Other Buildings

Drakes Place at Rhydd

Drakes Place, at Rhydd, is seen (2.17) c.1910, when it was owned by Capt Allen and his family. The occasion is a Croome Hunt meet, with servants providing refreshment. Capt Allen may be the gentleman in the doorway. It is a very evocative picture of a way of life that has largely passed, though hunting survives. In 1973-74, the Croome Hunt amalgamated with the West Warwickshire Farmers Hunt, and became known as the 'Croome and West Warwickshire Hunt'.

The house, which had extensive waterfront on the River Severn, was burnt down in 1958-59 and replaced by a much smaller structure of wooden frame, which was occupied by local solicitor, Bob Mayhew in 1960-61, until his death in 2005.

The present building, which replaced Mr Mayhew's house, is substantially larger. The original cellars contained three 'igloo' ice houses and were only filled in during this most recent rebuilding. The outbuildings are now converted into separate dwellings. The old dairy was converted and is occupied by Ian Seward, the son of retired Parish Councillor Pauline Cooper. Ian's son, Eric, is the craftsman responsible for the 2008 replacement of the Village Hall windows with hardwood double-glazed windows.

Figure 2.17 Drakes Place at Rhydd.

The Malt House and Village Hall

The building, which now houses the Village Hall and the adjacent former Men's Club, began life as a Malt House in about 1870. Malting for the brewing industry was at that time undertaken on a small scale, processing local farmers' barley. The malting process involved steeping the barley grains in large tanks of water, after which the barley was spread on the floor, five inches deep, where the barley would be allowed to germinate, and where it was turned regularly by hand. Germination was halted at the "green malt" stage, and was taken through the kilning process, which dried it and gave colour to the grain. It is probable that germination took place on the large area of floor of the main hall, and kilning in the tallest part of the building.

Malting ceased by 1911, and the building was unused for several years. In 1922, the premises were purchased by the newly-formed Parish Club Committee with money raised by public subscription, augmented by a mortgage from a local building society. Commander F J Ratcliff RN (retired) acted as sponsor and guarantor for the loan. 'The Parish Club' become known as 'The Guarlford Men's Club', and in 1931, being the only regular tenant, the Men's Club gradually took control of the whole of the building except Malt House Cottage; the Club's sign, much weathered, can still be seen high up on the wall outside.

During the Second World War, the larger upper room was let separately to Messrs Winwood as a Furniture Repository, and the income from the letting to Winwoods enabled the club to pay off the mortgage on the whole building. The Men's Club continued to meet throughout the war in its original part of the building which was locked off from the hall. After the war, the Club decided to make the hall available for public use, as had originally been intended at the time of purchase in 1922. Subsequently, the first Parish Hall Committee was appointed, and in September 1946 'Guarlford Village Hall' was opened by Countess Beauchamp, wife of the 8th and final Earl. The Men's Club continued to use part of the building until it closed because of dwindling membership in the mid-1980s; that part of the building has since been sold and is due for restoration. The Village Hall, on the other hand, has benefited from successive repairs and improvements and more are planned.

Figure 2.18 (Above) The Men's Club.   (Angus McCulloch).

View of the former Men's Club from the entrance to Penny Lane. The Village Hall roof behind is visible on the right, and the Malthouse Cottage is on the left hand side of the picture.

Figure 2.19 (Top right) An early view of Malthouse Cottage.

Figure 2.20 (Bottom Right) The Village Hall.   (Michael Skinner).

The Village Hall entrance, showing the new disabled access ramp installed to conform with the Disability Discrimination Act of 2004.

Converted Barns

Heriots Farm

With some exceptions perhaps, old farm buildings are no longer suitable for modern use. Most farms in the parish, before the trend to specialise after the Second World War, had a range of buildings for many different animals and crops. They had a few pig sties, a shed for calves, a fold yard for cattle in winter, and stables for work horses. Most had an old parlour where cows were milked, and a barn for storing corn in sacks, and hay and straw in ricks. Some farms, such as New House Farm, had hop kilns, and although the last of the hopyards in the parish was dismantled before the Second World War, the kilns remain today, like many of the other old buildings. With the modern scale of farming, where machinery replaces much of the labour, amalgamated farms now have large new, purpose-built buildings.

Some old farm buildings were removed and replaced by modern sheds some time ago. Others have more recently been converted to dwellings, as their potential to create houses with character in lovely rural settings was recognised. The big hay barn at 'The Heriots', for instance, was converted to living accommodation alongside the farmhouse in 1986, and is now the home of Peter and Carol Murphy. The interior of the original barn and the magnificent timbers are shown (2.21). Timbers used to build farm buildings were said to be much older than the barns in many cases, as they were regularly recovered and re-used when old ships were dismantled. The water tank was set high up amongst the rafters, into which the well water was pumped; and it was from this high point that the water was gravity-fed to the house, dairy and drinking troughs. An unusual view (2.22) gives a glimpse of the field and hedge behind the barn; while Peter and Carol are standing outside the windows which replaced the big doorway (2.23) in the third photograph. One house was created from the three cottages which stood by the original farmhouse. These cottages were sold by Madresfield Estate in the big estate sale of 1919.

Figure 2.21 (Left) Barn Interior.   *Figure 2.22 (Top) Barn Exterior.*   *Figure 2.23 (Bottom) Converted Barn.*   *(Peter Mayner).*

Lost Cottages

Jessamine, Lashford and Hall Green Cottages

Guarlford had a number of old cottages, many of them black and white, which have now gone. Alec Clifton-Taylor says in Pevsner's *Worcestershire*, 1968, "Worcestershire's half-timbering is now almost all of the 'black-and-white' kind characteristic of every county of the West Midlands." p.50. The Foley Estate replaced many of its own black and white cottages with brick cottages, considered to provide much better accommodation than the black and white cottages which had little or no foundations, and were no doubt originally cold and draughty homes. Over the years, many cottages have been renovated or have been significantly changed, with brick extensions. Some cottages were demolished and not replaced.

The black and white cottage (2.24) was one of two detached cottages in Clevelode Lane opposite what is now A J Gammond Ltd's yard. In 1910, George and Rose Sims and their family lived in the cottage nearest the junction with the Upton on Severn-Callow End road. This photograph shows Rose Sims with their children, Hilda, who was ten years old, and Fanny, Tom, and twins, Bill and Rose. William Sims and his wife lived next door until 1915, with their three daughters and son Bill, (known as 'Doodey').

Jessamine and Lashford Cottages (2.25) stood opposite the 'Green Dragon'. These were sold for £235 in the Foley Estate sale in 1910. When they were demolished, no replacements were built on the site.

Mrs Williams, Miss Williams and Mrs Bedington are seen (2.26) outside three cottages at Hall Green in 1900. These were later demolished and replaced by 'The Paddocks'.

Figure 2.24 (Opposite left) The Sims's Cottage.

Figure 2.25 (Top right) Jessamine and Lashford Cottages.

Figure 2.26 (Bottom right) Hall Green Cottages.

Modern Houses

Bamford Close, Penny Lane and Penny Close

Figure 2.27 Bamford Close, 2007.   (Michael Skinner).

Figure 2.28 (Top left) Penny Close, 2007.   (Michael Skinner).

Built after the Second World War to house agricultural workers, now largely owner-occupied.

Figure 2.29 (Top right) Bamford Close, 1971.   (Michael Skinner).

This group of eleven timber framed houses and the smaller group in Penny Lane were completed in 1972. Here Amanda and Sara Skinner can be seen inspecting their future home; in the background can be seen one of the other houses near completion.

Figure 2.30 (Left) The front view of the house before the scaffolding was put up. This view shows the Scots pines behind the house, on the border of Cherry Orchard.   (Michael Skinner).

Chapter 3

The Guarlford National School

Introduction

Phyl Bayliss said "I loved Guarlford School; I didn't want to leave a bit!", talking about her time at the village school from 1921 to 1930, words echoed by many of the pupils who appear in the following photographs. With the church, the village school was at the heart of the community's life in this parish and in parishes throughout the land, an historical fact for which there is ample pictorial and verbal testimony. In this county, for example, *Worcestershire Within Living Memory*, a 1995 compilation by the Worcestershire Federation of Women's Institutes, has an evocative section of images and memories from schooldays in the first half of the twentieth century.

According to the available evidence, Guarlford National School was built in 1867. From the beginning of the nineteenth century, charitable bodies, such as the British and Foreign Bible Society and the National Society for the Education of the Poor, were establishing schools; and in 1861 a Commission had recommended that local Boards of Education should be created. These Boards would collect a 'school rate' and build schools to improve the educational standard of the population as a whole. It was only in 1880 that an Education Act made school attendance compulsory for children up to the age of ten years; by the end of the century, the compulsory school-leaving age was twelve years and education was free for all children.

Much of what is told about the village school in this chapter comes from the one remaining School Log Book, covering the period from 1900 to 1946, as well as from the memories of those who spent their important and formative years at Guarlford National School.

The School and School House

This photograph of Guarlford National School and the attached three-bedroomed 'School House' was taken in the 1970s. The school itself consisted of one large classroom and a smaller room for the Infants. The large room was divided in two by a curtain, and tortoise stoves warmed the rooms. The building was erected on land between the church and the Rectory, land which had been given by Mr Edward Foley in 1843, and stood side-on to the lane. The school itself and the 'School House' are described in more detail in Chapter Six of *The Guarlford Story*. The Woolley family were occupants of the house for many years, and Mrs Woolley continued to live there until 1971, long after the death of her husband, who had been Headmaster, in 1941.

The old school buildings were finally demolished in the 1970s, and a pair of semi-detached houses now stand on the site in Rectory Lane, formerly 'Cherry Orchard Lane'. Both the School House and the old name of the lane are perpetuated, the former in the name 'Old School House' given to the home now on the site and the latter on the sign facing the church. Thus earlier times are recalled.

Figure 3.1 The School and School House, Rectory Lane.

The Class of 1900

The entry in the School Log Book for 5th February, 1900, says "I commenced duties as master this morning"; and so Mr Alfred Ernest Martin began his long career as Headmaster of Guarlford School. The 1901 Census describes him as "Schoolmaster", aged forty-two, and having been born in Nottingham. Also recorded in the Census are his wife, Louisa, aged twenty-five, born in Steeple Claydon, Buckinghamshire, and daughters, Margaret, aged two, also born in Steeple Claydon, and Gwendolyn, aged one, born in Guarlford. Sadly, however, there is a record of a Gwendolyn Louisa Martin whose death, aged thirteen, was recorded with the Upton Registrar in March, 1913.

In this photograph from 1900, all the staff and pupils are standing in the playground to the left of the school buildings. Mr and Mrs Martin are in the back row towards the left. The redbrick wall seen here still stands in 2008.

Note the girls' pinafores and the sturdy boots worn by all the children. Most of the children face forward for the serious business of the photograph, but, perhaps inevitably, a few have been distracted and have turned away at the vital moment.

The 'catchment area' was large – something perhaps reflected in the size of the group – and many children walked across fields and along muddy lanes to get to school. Moreover, the Log Book records snow and floods soon after Mr Martin arrived.

The Aid Grants, which depended on good reports from the Inspectors, were £20 in December, 1900, and December, 1901.

When the School Log Book begins in 1900, the accommodation in the classrooms is described as "Mixed School 70" and "Infants 50", thus allowing for 120 pupils. However, not all the pupils attended all the time. Reference is made on several occasions to the bad attendance record. For example, on 24th July, 1903, an Attendance Officer visited the School – and on 28th July, 112 of the 122 pupils on the register attended School, "the highest number for some time"!

Mr Martin taught the Mixed Class, which had children of all abilities between the ages of seven and thirteen (later fourteen) years.

Figure 3.2 The Class of 1900.

Miss Price and the Class of 1910

Mrs Martin took charge of the Infants and Standard One, although the Standard One children later moved into the Mixed Class. Mrs Martin was helped by a monitress and then by an assistant teacher. Miss Florence Ada Price is pictured here in 1910 as an assistant teacher. In June, 1913, Florence married Victor Bradshaw, son of Mr and Mrs Absalom Bradshaw of Guarlford Court, and the young couple made their home at White House Farm, where their daughter, Joan Bradshaw, was born.

Florence looks very elegant with her blouse sleeves in the 'leg o'mutton' style which had been popular in past years. She has a gentle smile in the photograph, but her children look somewhat overcome by the solemnity of the occasion. Again, stout footwear is in evidence.

On 19th August, 1910, the School Log Book records a great improvement to the school building, when small windows were added and "the hoppering provides inlets for fresh air". In March, 1910, the same Log Book had reported that the air in the classrooms was full of dust because of the lack of good ventilation.

Figure 3.3 Miss Price and the Class of 1910.

The Class of 1912

This photograph was taken beside the boys' entrance to the School buildings, with the churchyard in the background. Mrs Martin is shown here with her Standard One Infants Class. Note the clothes of the children: several are obviously sisters and, once more, the pinafores are still very much in evidence, as are the boots.

A particular feature of this picture is the church bell hanging in the hornbeam tree in the churchyard, where it still remains to this day over a century after its 'temporary' removal from the church. The bell was an irresistible target for young boys for many decades! This class photograph has quite an autumnal setting, with bare branches and fallen leaves suggesting the beginning of the school year. In less than two years' time the families of these children would have their lives overshadowed by World War.

Figure 3.4 The Class of 1912.

The Classes of 1913 and the1920s

The next three photographs are of school groups taken in 1913 and the 1920s.

The little girls of 1913 in (3.5) are still wearing pinafores, obviously their 'Sunday best' in some cases, and boots are still necessary - and very dusty in this picture. Note the little girl in black on the left, who looks as if she may be in mourning. According to the records, the Martins probably lost a child, Gwendolyn, in 1913, and there is also a reference in the School Log Book to the death of another daughter, Mina, on 4th March, 1919. (The death of a Wilhelmina E. Martin, aged seven, was indeed registered in Upton-upon-Severn at that time.) Great sadness then for the couple, who would also have to cope with the worries of children who had fathers and brothers fighting in the First World War. More about the role of Guarlford School in the Great War can be found on pages 131 and 135 of *The Guarlford Story*.

In the group photograph (3.6) of the class of 1920, Milly Young appears standing to the right of Mrs Martin. Milly was the sister of Mark Young, who established the smithy on the Guarlford Road not far from Mill Farm. She was also for a time Joan Bradshaw's nurse. The little girl, fifth from the right in the front row, is Alice Neal.

The windows' 'hoppering', installed in 1910, is apparently being put to good use in both this picture and the following one.

Mr and Mrs Martin are seen c.1920 (3.7) with an older group of scholars, some of whom were probably ready to leave school.

(In this instance, the year of the photograph does not appear to be written on the blackboard.)

The 1918 Education Act raised the school leaving age to fourteen, which must have proved annoying to some youngsters, especially as, during the First World War, according to an entry in the Log Book in April, 1915, all the boys over twelve years of age, except one, had been given leave to go to work on the farms. By June, 1915, even younger boys were helping to replace the agricultural workers who had been conscripted into His Majesty's Forces.

Figure 3.5 The Class of 1913.

Figure 3.6 Mr and Mrs Martin and The Class of 1920.

Figure 3.7 Mr and Mrs Martin and the Class of c.1920.

The Class of 1922

Two who are girls still remembered in the village today appear in this photograph: Phyl Bayliss (nee Bedington) and Rene Sims (nee Waters) are seated second and third from the right. The two were lifelong friends, a friendship which began in Guarlford National School. It is noticeable that the children, and the girls in particular, are now wearing much more modern clothes and no pinafores, although it seems that the strong boots are still a necessity.

Mr and Mrs Martin left Guarlford National School in January, 1923, and a Dora Gardner was temporarily in charge until the next Headmaster, and his family, arrived in April of that year.

Figure 3.8 The Class of c.1922.

The Class of 1928-1929

Back Row

Mr Clarence Woolley; Goff Powell; Nina Brush, later Mrs Bernard Clarke, mother of Daphne Hayes; Joan Bradshaw; Monica Woolley; Lucy Brush, later Mrs Panting; Archie Pritchard.

Middle Row

George Waldwyn; Phyl Bedington, later Mrs Owen Bayliss; Muriel King; Thelma Ackerman, granddaughter of Mrs Thomas of the Tan House; Rene Waters, later Mrs Sims; Phyllis Harris(?); Winnie Waldwyn; Dolly Yapp(?); David Woolley.

Front Row

Lily Clark; Enid Rogers; Amy Neal; Jessie Little (?); Curly Jones, later Mrs Hatt; Dorothy Hawker; Dossie Williams.

The members of this happy group have been identified by various people. Perhaps there is a little less reserve and formality about having a school photograph taken now and there seems to be a greater variety in children's clothes.

Mr Clarence William Woolley took up his post as Headmaster on 16th April, 1923. He is described as a "kindly disciplinarian", and his pupils speak of him with affection. He and his wife lived with their six children in the School House. Monica Woolley, shown here in the back row, became a teacher also, and many in Malvern will remember her teaching at Malvern Parish School.

Figure 3.9 Mr Woolley and the Class of 1928-29.

Miss Cope and the Class of c.1930

Back Row

Miss Cope; unknown; Ray Barrett; Charles Bladder; unknown; Sam Beard; unknown.

Middle Row

Third left John Bedington; first girl Linda Morris; last two Colin Bradshaw and Ernie Clarke.

Front Row, seated:

George Fisher; Joyce Clark; unknown; unknown; unknown; Edgar Bateman.

All that is known of Miss Cope, teacher of the Juniors in the 1930s, is that she was the daughter of a police Inspector from Upton-upon-Severn.

Figure 3.10 Miss Cope and the Class of c.1930.

Mr Woolley and the Class of 1935

Derrick Bladder stands tall in the middle of the back row of pupils, in this photograph from 1935, together with Mr Woolley and the rest of the class. John Bedington is on the far right. The church porch can be seen in the background.

The children were very familiar with St Mary's Church in Guarlford, as they would attend Services there from time to time, such as the Memorial Service on 28th January, 1936, to mark the funeral of George V. The School Log Book also records that on 11th November, 1935, "All pupils above Standard One marched to the Memorial Cross on Armistice Day."

Figure 3.11 Mr Woolley and the Class of 1935.

Miss Cole and the Class of 1935

Pamela Fairhurst (nee Newson) described her first experiences of school thus: "One small room, which was my world – the Infants room – presided over by one of life's natural teachers, Hilda Cole, who taught generations of children to read and write and made it all seem like fun. And oh, the wonderful smell of the corner cupboard full of plasticine, blunt scissors, raffia, beads etc., which came out after all the hard work had been finished – and the lovely round stove which gave out a tremendous heat and was surrounded by a circular guard to stop little hands getting burned. We won't dwell on the outside lavatories, the girls off one playground and the boys off another, cold, miserable but necessary places."

As perhaps we would expect, there are consistent threads running through the remembered experiences of childhood, and of school, in particular. Laurie Lee, for example, recalls the smells of the classroom in *Cider with Rosie*, p. 53; and the stove that gave out "tremendous heat" is also a recurring vivid memory, and understandably so in cold classrooms before central heating.

Miss Cole does indeed seem to have been a 'natural teacher'. She was the daughter of Mr Cole, the wheelwright in Chance Lane, and started teaching the Infants on 19th November, 1920. Her sister, Marjory, was also an assistant teacher at Guarlford National School, but she died on 10th October, 1923, aged only 20 years.

His Majesty's Inspectors reported on visits to the school on 3rd and 4th July, 1924, saying that "The Infants are making satisfactory progress. Their teacher recently spent a month in a school where free methods are in use, and she has profited greatly from the experience."

Also in the photograph, standing front left, is Mr Woolley's younger daughter, Margaret, "all knobbly knees and gappy smile" (Margaret's own description of herself).

Figure 3.12 Miss Cole and the Class of 1935.

Miss Cole and the Class of 1938

Back Row
Miss Cole; Harry Bladder; Bob Tustin; unknown; unknown; Stan Jackson.

Middle Row
Edwin Lane; Vic Vivian; Hilda Powell; Doreen Clarke; Joy Clark; John Little; Bill Cooper.

Front Row
Joan Warwick; Rona Sims; Mary Little; Margaret Yapp; Orlean Whitlock.

Another happy group of Guarlford children is seen here with their teacher, Miss Hilda Cole. These later group photographs show the children looking noticeably more relaxed than in those taken at the beginning of the century. Perhaps this has to do both with the greater familiarity of photography and with the changed social climate. This is a slightly smaller group than in 1930, and this may have had significance for the school's future.

The school buildings had begun to deteriorate and Mr Woolley was not well and was to die of kidney failure in 1941. At this time the authorities were considering closing Guarlford School and moving the children to Madresfield. However, with another war looming, it was thought that Guarlford School should stay open to accommodate the expected evacuees to the village.

The children here grew up sharing their school with children who came mostly from Selly Oak, including Reg Bevan who has very fond memories of the five years he spent in Guarlford, saying that: "Miss Cole used to take us for country-dance lessons out in the playground. I used to think the dancing was a bit daft, although I preferred it to trying to do sums, but I enjoyed the tunes. Two have stuck with me to this day; I have had a lifelong love of traditional music, thanks to Miss Cole and her dancing lessons."

Figure 3.13. Miss Cole and the Class of 1938.

Miss Cole at Madresfield School c.1950

The final photograph in this chapter was not taken in Guarlford but in Madresfield in the early 1950s.
With Miss Cole are some children from Guarlford.

Back Row
Miss Cole; unknown; unknown; Clifford Hayes; unknown; unknown; Michael Meek; unknown; Jimmy Hewston.

Front Row
unknown; unknown; unknown; Betty Little; Kay Halward; unknown; unknown; unknown; Daphne Hayes, nee Clarke; unknown.

On 2nd October, 1944, sixteen children from Guarlford, between the ages of seven and eleven years of age, were entered onto the Register at Madresfield School, among them three evacuees who later returned to Birmingham. Other pupils, having reached the age of eleven plus, had moved on to secondary education elsewhere, leaving just fourteen Infants at Guarlford School in the care of Miss Cole. The Guarlford School Log Book ends on 16th January, 1946, but nowhere is there any record of exactly when Guarlford National School closed. However, the Madresfield School Register records the fact that on 2nd April, 1946, ten children from Guarlford, between the ages of five and seven years, were enrolled at Madresfield. Money raised by the sale of Guarlford School was used to improve the facilities at Madresfield. Miss Cole rejoined her pupils when, after being interviewed in November, 1946, she was appointed as an assistant teacher at Madresfield School. The school bus collected pupils from the end of Chance Lane, where Miss Cole lived; and if it did not arrive, she would escort the children on foot along the lane to Madresfield, something that is hard to envisage happening now in the twenty-first century. Miss Cole married Mr Cyril Wall on 10th August, 1957.

Mrs Hilda Mary Wall (nee Cole) died on 2nd December, 1976. She is buried in Madresfield churchyard, appropriately perhaps, facing the school where she taught the last of her pupils from Guarlford.

Figure 3.14 Miss Cole at Madresfield School in the early 1950s.

Chapter 4

The Guarlford Football Club

Introduction

In common with villages and towns throughout the country, Guarlford has been part of what amounts to a long British tradition and one which has made a significant contribution to community pride and identity. The twentieth century saw football in Guarlford become a sport played and supported by a cross-section of the village population over seven decades, with the ups and downs of success familiar perhaps to all clubs and all who follow their varying fortunes. National rules and the advent of the 'Football Association' in 1863 gave the sport an impetus which led nearly half a century later to the formation of Guarlford's own amateur team.

According to Joan Bradshaw's notes, the first Guarlford Football Club was formed on 7th October, 1907. The kit at that time consisted of a white shirt and a green sash. In later decades, the colours of the team kit were blue and white. The Captain in 1907 was Bob Stanton, and Oliver Victor Bradshaw was the Honorary Secretary. The team played its inaugural match on 26th October that year on a field at Guarlford Court, and the farm granary was used as a changing room. The Club's Minutes of that time record thanks for gifts of "goals and field from Messrs Bladder and Medcalf".

An article about the history of Guarlford Football Club appeared in the *Malvern Gazette* on 28th April, 1966, which stated that the club had been "formed in 1919". However, it seems that the original Club, founded in 1907, had disbanded at the onset of the First World War and re-formed in peacetime.

Evidently, the Football Club had plenty of loyal support in the parish over the years, with local farmers, such as the Bullocks, the Bradshaws, the Medcalfs of New House Farm, the Bladders of Fowler's Farm, and the Lanes of Woodbridge Farm, providing grounds and equipment. For a long time, Cdr Ratcliff, as President, and others helped financially, and many villagers actively supported the team as players and spectators.

Autumn Oak by Tom Vivian.

The 1920s

The *Malvern Gazette* article of 1966 says about the Club: "Among the Malvern League Clubs, Guarlford has one of the most interesting histories. The Club joined the Malvern League twice and also competed in the Upton League before the (Second World) War. After playing friendly matches in their first season after the First World War, the villagers joined the Malvern League when it was formed in the 1920-21 season. With no major successes under their belts, they joined the Upton League in 1927 - that season...they failed to win a match and finished bottom."

This photograph was taken after the 1919–1920 season, as can be seen from the helpful writing on the football, which is held by Arthur Shinn of Guarlford Road, sitting cross-legged in the middle of the front row.

On the far right of the front row is Frank Jarrett, a popular team member from Hanley Swan, who is remembered not only as driving the butcher's cart "... in a spotless white coat and blue striped apron", but also as a talented pianist and band leader at many a village dance.

Standing with the players in the back row are active supporters from the village: George Beard and the Revd F Newson on the left and George Lane of Woodbridge Farm second from the right.

According to the Club's minutes book of 1923, sawdust was used to mark out the pitch – later it was lime - and the team were transported to away matches in lorries. Entertainment tax was levied on gate returns for soccer and rugby clubs at this time, and in October, 1923, admission charges were set as follows: "All men and boys who had left school to pay five pence. All ladies and children still at school three pence." In 1923–24, the team used 'Mr Bullock's meadow'. There is also a story that they later used a hut at the 'Green Dragon' as a changing room for a while.

The trainer carried a first aid case, and in December, 1924, the committee decided that half a crown's worth of brandy should be included in the contents.

Throughout the existence of the Football Club, the women of the village were very supportive, washing the kit and cleaning the changing room. There are also references over the years to a Ladies' Committee, which provided refreshments for whist drives and dances, sometimes organising events themselves to raise funds for the Club.

Figure 4.1 The 1919-20 Team.   *(C D Walton).*

The 1930s

According to various history notes, in the 1929-30 season Guarlford Football Club did much better than a year or two earlier, winning the Upton League Championship and the Gresson Cup. At this time, Mr Rod Vivian of Blakes Lane was Club Secretary. Mr Vivian and his son, Victor, served the Club loyally and practically in various offices over many years.

In the 1930–31 season the team again won the Upton League and also the Cowley Cup, finishing runners-up in 1932, when they rejoined the Malvern League. This photograph, which was taken in the grounds of the Rectory, shows the triumphant team with two cups (possibly those won that season). Once again, Mr Arthur Shinn is seated in the centre of the picture, holding the football with the dates painted on. At the far right of the front row is Mr George Lane.

The team reached the 1936 final of the King George V Jubilee Competition, losing 2-1 to Holy Trinity. The following season they won the Malvern League.

Modern footballers should note the football boots and heavy leather football. Before 1836, footballs consisted of animal bladders with a covering made of leather, and p. 60 of *The Guarlford Story* describes how pigs' bladders were used as footballs by the children. Pigs' bladders in footballs were replaced by vulcanised rubber bladders in the mid nineteenth century.

In 1863, the rule was established that a match football "... must be spherical with a circumference of 27 to 28 inches (68.6 – 71.1 cms)." This is still the regulation size of a football, as set down in the FIFA Rules of 2007. However, the regulation weight has changed, increasing from 13 to 15 ozs to 14 to 16 ozs.

Leather balls were good for kicking, but very painful when heading, as recalled by Derrick Bladder, a member of the Guarlford Football Club teams after the Second World War. The weight of the ball was not helped by the heavy stitching and the water absorption of the leather. By the 1980s, synthetic 'leather' was being used to manufacture footballs, a material with less water absorption and made of shaped patches sewn together.

Figure 4.2 The 1930-31 Team.

1937-1938

The team had a very successful season in 1937–38, when they won two major cups – the Malvern League and the Hospital Senior Cup. This photograph shows the team with three cups, as they also won the Hospital Secondary Cup that year.

The total time taken for Guarlford FC's Hospital Cup Final versus Newtown FC set a record. The score after the ninety-minute Final was drawn at 2-all. Then there was a replay match lasting ninety minutes, score 1-1; after extra time it was 2–2. A second replay followed with no score at full-time, and 1–1 after extra time. Guarlford finally won 3–1 after a further 7 minutes each way. The total time for the tie was 345 minutes!

However, in the next season the team went down in the Senior Cup Final, losing 4–1 to West Malvern, who then held the cup throughout the war years when no competitive local football was played.

Mrs Phyl Bayliss was very proud of the football team, and in 2004 she recalled many of those in the team and their supporters in the late thirties:

"My Owen (Phyllis's husband) was in the Guarlford Football Team; one year they won three cups in one season. Owen's family lived in Hanley Swan, and I met him when I watched Guarlford play football and he was in the team. He worked at a farm in Hanley for thirteen years and then at Mr Bakewell's (Grove House Farm) for twenty-nine years. There were Owen and his brother, who also lived at Hanley; two Davises from Callow End; the blacksmith from Barnard's Green; Gussy Holt; John Woolley from the school, the eldest son of the Headmaster; 'Sunshine' Carty the goalkeeper; Mr Jones from Hanley; someone called Brown, a Lowe, a Dovey; two young boys called Phipps from Hanley. Supporters were: Mr Beard and Cdr Ratcliff, who lived at Dripshill; Mr George Lane, Edwin's uncle, and Ted Amory; Mr Tommy Clark (his house is gone now), and Mr Wilks, who lived at the farm along the bottom road. The team wore blue shirts with white sleeves."

Identified in this photograph are: in the back row, standing second, third and fourth from left respectively, Mr George Beard, Mr George Lane and Cdr Ratcliff. Third from right is 'Sunshine' Carty. Seated second from left in the middle row is John Woolley, and Owen Bayliss and his brother, known as 'Chum', are second and third from left in the front row. The two young boys are called Phipps, related to the Hanley Swan butchers.

Figure 4.3 The 1937-38 Team.

1948-1954

The *Malvern Gazette* described this period as Guarlford FC's "golden era". The Club had been re-started after the Second World War, when a public meeting was called, and Mr George Lane, who had been the Chairman and Treasurer before the War, handed over the Club funds totalling £6 7s 6d, which he had kept safely in a cocoa tin.

Evidently, between 1948 and 1954, Guarlford FC did indeed have many successes, winning the Worcestershire Minor Cup, the Ogilvy Cup and the Auxiliary Fire Service Cup once, and the League, Senior Cup and Secondary Cups twice.

This photograph was taken after the team won the County Minor Cup in 1950 and shows:

Back row, left to right: George Beard; A Neale; Derrick Bladder; Mr Skillern; Charles Bladder; J Bingham; D Young; Owen Bayliss; Unknown.

Front row, left to right: T R Jones; T Jones; E Stallard; H Stallard; J Smith. (Messrs Bayliss, Beard and Medcalf were longstanding supporters of the team.)

The *Malvern Gazette* of Friday 14th April, 1950, described the conditions that day:

"County Minor Cup stays in Malvern - Lone Goal Win for Guarlford in Gusty Final.

A few minutes calm in the boisterous wind conditions on Saturday enabled E Stallard to score for Guarlford and so bring the Worcestershire Minor Cup to Malvern for the second year in succession at the expense of Bell United, who were defeated by the only goal scored in the ninety minutes play. Great interest had been aroused by the fixture, a crowd of 1,000 attending, many of whom wore either the blue and white or green favours of the teams... Throughout the game – with the exception of one short spell of ten minutes during which the Malvern side netted – a high wind made ball control an exceptionally hazardous job for the players. So much so that neither side were able to take advantage to the full extent of early moves, the ball often being carried by the wind far off the field of play."

Incidentally, a reminder of how long rationing continued after the Second World War is shown in the minutes of 1950, when reference is made to having to apply for an allocation from the local Food Office for rations in order to buy items for half-time refreshments.

Figure 4.4 The 1950 Team.

1955-1956

This photograph from the 1955–56 season was taken in a field on New House Farm provided for the Club for many decades by the Medcalf family, and still known as 'the Football Field'. Dripshill can be seen in the background.

In the photograph are: in the back row, A Neale; N Brown; Charles Bladder; T Jones; A K Phipps; R Yates; and in the front row, L Dance; Mr Davis; J Holt; H Stallard and B Preece.

Charles Bladder is still remembered in the village today for his long association with Guarlford FC. He had also been selected to play for The Malverns XI against The Army in 1954 at Langland Stadium, when the newspaper report commented on the "superb Malverns half-back line of Saunders, Bladder and Horton". The Malverns XI won 3–1.

Here are two newspaper reports about Charles, the first from *The Evening News and Times* of Saturday 31st May, 1952:

"Henry Charles Bladder, 32, a motor-cyclist, of The Glen, Guarlford, captain and secretary of the Guarlford Football Club, is detained in Worcester Royal Infirmary with an injured ankle received yesterday while negotiating a bend on the Old Hills. Mr Bladder, who was travelling towards Worcester, had slowed down on the bend for a flock of geese when the footrest of a motor-cycle following him caught his ankle as the machine was overtaking him."

This injury did affect Charles's football playing for a while, but not permanently, as can be seen from this cutting from *The Saturday Sports News* of 28th May, 1955:

"It was a very happy atmosphere that prevailed at the end-of-season supper of Guarlford FC, held last weekend at Guarlford Village Hall. The only jarring note was the information that next season the club will have to find a new secretary. For the last 10 years or so Mr Charles Bladder has filled this office with distinction. He is to be married in June and feels that he must relinquish the secretaryship, but this does not mean that he will sever his connection with the club.

In fact I would not be in the least surprised if next season Charles is again occasionally seen filling the centre-half position in the Guarlford team."

(A note is attached to the cutting: "Charles carried on playing until 1965 and acting on Committee for several years after hanging up his boots.")

Figure 4.5 The 1955 Team.

Miss Guarlford

The first reference in the club minutes to a 'Beauty Queen Competition' is in December, 1952, when the members of the committee were planning a dance for Friday 6th February, 1953 (Coronation Year). According to the minutes, the 'Beauty Queen' that year was Miss Jean Williams, and in 1954 Mrs D M Young was chosen.

'Miss Guarlford 1955', pictured in this photograph, was a Miss J Clements of Upton-upon-Severn. At the Annual Dinner on 18th February, 1955, she was selected as 'Miss Guarlford' for the 'Malvern Football Queen Competition', the winner of which would ride on a float in the summer Carnival procession. The photograph was published in the *Saturday Sports News*, a companion paper to the *Malvern Gazette* and the *Worcester News*, on February 26th, 1955. The newspaper was also known as the *'Green'un'*, and the cutting from which this information comes is indeed of green paper.

In the photograph are: left to right, Victor Vivian; Rod Vivian; John Attwood; Charles Bladder; Mrs Betty Brown; Miss J Clements; Dr Alec Brown; Mrs Francis Thomas; (someone unknown peeping through); George Thomas and the Reverend Frederick Newson.

Father and son, Rod and Victor Vivian, of course, are remembered for serving Guarlford Football Club very well over many years and in many ways.

Mr Attwood, of Kennel Cottage, Rhydd, was the Club Chairman at this time. He was a policeman who had retired from the Gloucestershire Constabulary in September, 1938, moved to Guarlford and then became a round rick builder and thatcher. His daughter, Muriel, married Alan Webb, and they farmed Portocks End Farm. Charles Bladder was the Club Secretary. Dr and Mrs Brown and Mr and Mrs Thomas were judges for the competition. The four were acquainted with Mrs Newson through the St John Ambulance Brigade. Dr Brown practised at the Avenue Road Surgery, and Mr Thomas was the pharmacist of Claremont Pharmacy, Church Street, Great Malvern.

Much planning went into social events for the Football Club, which seems to have been not just a sports team but also an important part of village life. The immediately following decades saw the decline and virtual disappearance of such very local clubs, as well as other societies, in Guarlford and comparable villages.

Figure 4.6 Miss Guarlford at the Football Club Dinner.

1972

This photograph was taken at the Malvern Town Football Club Ground, Langlands, in 1972.

In the back row are: Alan Clifton; Brian Macey; Rod Vivian (Chairman); Chris Lowe; Kevin Shepherd; Mick Churchill; Tony Crease; John Bilbeck.

In the front row: Mr Campbell; Ken Richards; Don Loader; Mick Bradford; John Cartwright.

There are not many more records presently available about the Guarlford Football Club. The 28th April, 1966, article in the *Malvern Gazette* refers to the team being relegated to Division Two in 1954, but then gaining promotion to the First Division in 1965, when Guarlford won the Mason and Supplementary Cups.

Captain of the team at that time was John Yapp, who had played football while in the Guards and had "turned out in the club's blue and white stripes for three years".

Those in the team shown in this photograph still have memories of playing for Guarlford FC. For example, Brian Macey (in the back row) recalls having to check that the playing field in Guarlford was clear of cow pats before matches began, and he also remembers the victorious match depicted here.

It seems, however, that the football team ceased playing some time soon after 1972, but in its decades of history the various members of the Guarlford FC were important in the life of the village, enjoying the support of the community and, we are told, providing much entertainment.

Figure 4.7 The 1972 Team.

Chapter 5

Village Life

Introduction

For countless generations village life was the reality for the majority of the British population, and that life had a traditional character and rhythm; now such life is a dream for many who live in ever-growing towns and cities and long for a lost Eden of rural content. The garden cities and the widely spreading suburbs of the early twentieth century, for example, were a clear expression of this nostalgia for a rural past. However, for most who lived out their lives for centuries past in Britain's estimated ten thousand or more villages the reality was often hard and by no means altogether idyllic; though traditional rural life did not lack contentment and its pleasures.

Villages were made up of families who were usually church-goers and who worked and played together. Guarlford, like other English villages, was quite a close community, with families mingling socially and in sport, as well as working together on the land, while sometimes families came together also through marriage. In the twentieth century and on into the twenty-first, villages such as Guarlford still have their time–honoured occasions and ceremonies. Weddings and christenings, fetes, fancy dress competitions and seaside outings have all played their part here as elsewhere in bringing people together. More recently, two Royal Jubilees and a Millennium celebration have contributed to villagers' sense of shared identity as Guarlfordians; these occasions involving, too, relative newcomers to the village who wish to help maintain a sense of community. It is clear that village life is still valued and appreciated by those who live here, while Guarlford's local history project has itself helped to sustain village life by providing occasions for villagers to meet and learn more about the history of this place and its past inhabitants.

This chapter records some of the village's events of the last hundred years of dramatic change; but it can be seen to be change tempered by significant continuity.

St Mary's in the Snow by Keith Owen.

St Mary's, Guarlford

Until 1866, Malvern Priory was the parish church for the inhabitants of what is now Guarlford. The first stone of a Chapel of Ease, St Mary's, was laid by Lady Foley in 1843, and the chapel was completed the following year. It was subordinate to Malvern Priory and its purpose was to provide a nearer place of worship for the local population. In 1866, the Parish of Guarlford was formed and St Mary's then became its parish church. The first Rector was the Reverend John B Wathen.

A good indication of what the church looked like at that time can be gained from the photograph (5.1), which was taken sometime before 1906. Note the bell turret and the narrow alcoves in the west wall. The latter were built, it is assumed, to accommodate two narrow window lights at a later date. Note also the cross, which no longer exists, at the eastern end of the nave roof. Either side of the porch can be seen two small cedars. These grew to an enormous height and were felled in the early 1980s.

In 1877, there were two major additions to St Mary's: an organ chamber, now referred to as the outer vestry, which was built entirely at Lord Beauchamp's expense; and the installation of an organ at a cost of £180, expenditure met completely by public subscription.

In 1906, through the generosity of Lord Beauchamp, the west wall to the nave was partly dismantled and a large three-light stained glass window was installed which greatly improved the natural light within the church. During this work the bell turret was deemed to be unsafe and was not replaced. The bell, which was found to be cracked, was mounted temporarily in the nearby hornbeam tree (5.2). It was eventually re-cast in 1926, but no funds were ever raised to re-establish the turret. There is a more detailed account of the many other improvements to St Mary's in *The Guarlford Story*.

In the churchyard there once stood a graceful statue of the Madonna and child (5.3). This was a gift to Guarlford from the Reverend Osbourne Jay, late Vicar of Shoreditch, when he retired to Malvern. He taught boxing at his boys' club in London's East End and was known as 'The Boxing Parson'. The statue used to stand in his vicarage garden there. Sadly, it was stolen one night in 1991 and shortly afterwards the church gates, also in the photograph, were stolen. Replica gates were made jointly by Stephen Cooper and his woodwork tutor. Stephen was treasurer of Guarlford Parochial Church Council (PCC) for several years.

Figure 5.1 (Top left) St Mary's, pre 1906.   *Figure 5.2 (Right) The Church Bell.*   *Figure 5.3 (Bottom left) The Madonna and Child.*

Figure 5.4 (Opposite top left) A Palm Sunday Procession.

The Revd J Wathen and ladies taking part in a Palm Sunday procession of the early twentieth century.

Figure 5.5 (Opposite top right) Mrs Frances Newson.

Mrs Frances Newson, probably in the late 1920s or early 1930s, sitting on the famous 'Red Indian' motorcycle with sidecar she shared with her husband, the Reverend Frederick Newson. It is said that she could often be heard singing at the top of her voice as she sped along the country lanes. Later, the couple changed to a pony and trap before finally acquiring a motor car, believed to be a huge Riley, which, it is reported, Father Newson drove, dressed in his black robes, spats and biretta. Needless to say, all forms of transport at the Rectory were freely available for the benefit of everybody. From the day of her marriage in 1920, Frances May Newson became immersed in village life, fully supporting her husband with his pastoral care and getting involved in almost everything. During and following the Second World War, besides bringing up her family and taking in evacuee children, she served St John Ambulance with distinction, becoming Superintendent of the Malvern Division, and in 1980 she was appointed Commander of St John at a ceremony in the City of London. At her funeral at St Mary's in 1996, the St John Ambulance Malvern Division formed a Guard of Honour.

Figure 5.6 (Opposite bottom right) Rogation Sunday, c.1965.

The church congregation gathered outside Guarlford Court on Rogation Sunday. After the Rogation Service, the Revd Hartley Brown would then lead the congregation around the lanes in the vicinity of the church, blessing the fields as he went. This was probably a revised version of the ancient practice of 'beating the bounds'. It is reported that at the Harvest Supper later that year Mr Ron Smith, churchwarden, resplendent in three piece suit, watch chain and with fine moustache, commented to the assembled company that ever since Father Brown had sprinkled holy water on the fields it had done nothing but rain. This was a joke, but it is reported that Father Brown was not too sure.

Figure 5.7 (Opposite bottom left) Miss Helen Smith playing the organ.

Miss Helen Smith is at the organ in the 1980s. Helen, sister of Dorrie Smith, was a true friend and servant of St Mary's. For many years she played the organ at the weekly church services, freely giving her time, as well as faithfully carrying out the duties of sacristan, preparing the sacraments each week for communion services. Helen lived in Guarlford's aptly named 'Faith Cottage'

Figure 5.8 (Opposite top left) A Nativity Tableau at St Mary's, 1963-64.

From the left: Wendy Handy (angel); Maidie Bayliss (arms raised high as the angel Gabriel); Alison Smith, angel; unknown King; unknown small angel; Stephen Prosser, King; Ann Page, angel; Susan Medcalf, now Fellows, angel. What happened to the other players, we wonder.

Figure 5.9 (Opposite top right) Tapestry Kneelers.

In the mid 1980s, through the initiative of the Reverend David Martin, Rector at the time, the ladies of Guarlford embarked upon the production of the colourful tapestry kneelers in use to this day. From the left are: David Martin; Helen Smith; Mary Jones; and Mary Bruce. During his ministry as the first Rector of the combined parishes of Guarlford, Madresfield and Newland, David also introduced The Grapevine, the Combined Junior Church, the Youth Club and the Parish Singers.
(Reed Midland Newspapers, Hylton Road).

Figure 5.10 (Opposite bottom right) St Mary's Anniversary Reception.

1994 was the 150th anniversary of St Mary's. The event was celebrated with evensong in church followed by the planting of an oak tree in the churchyard by the Right Reverend Philip Goodrich,

Bishop of Worcester. Guest of Honour was Mrs Frances Newson. The photograph was taken at a reception in the Village Hall after the service. From the left: Clifford Hayes, Churchwarden; the Revd David Martin, former Rector; Mrs Frances Newson; the Right Revd Philip Goodrich; the Reverend Canon John Green, Rector; Bill Medcalf, former churchwarden; Ron Smith, former churchwarden; Meriel Smith, now Bennett, Churchwarden. Note the church vestments on display.

Figure 5.11 (Opposite bottom left) Tanzania.   (Barbara Hill).

In 1995, thanks to Canon John Green, then Priest-in-charge of Guarlford, Madresfield and Newland, and Mick and Val Levick, a Benefice link was established with the Diocese of Masasi in Tanzania. Initially, fund raising supported the maintenance of oxen for farming in Masasi, but later this was changed to funding a teacher in the Rondo Seminary. Each year to the present, at the annual parish Harvest Supper, sufficient donations have been raised to enable this funding to continue. In conjunction with a wider organisation 'Friends of Masasi', sufficient money was also raised to present a Land Rover for the use of the Masasi Diocese, an invaluable asset in a large diocese with very poor roads and little transport. In 1996, a party of six from the Benefice travelled to Masasi. The photograph, taken in a teak forest near Rondo, shows from the left:
Mick Levick; Land Rover driver, name lost; Val Levick; Stuart, Assistant Warden Rondo; Elizabeth Tidball; Forest Ranger, name lost; Don Hill; and John Green.

Figure 5.12 (Opposite top left) Sunday School Stamps from 1947.

These stamps were great incentives for regular attendance. Peter Titchener, who moved to Hall Green in 1953, recalled attending Sunday School every week so that he could collect his 'Never absent, never late' sticker for his book and ring the church bell.

Figure 5.13 (Opposite top right) The Sunday School Outing.

Sunday School outings and the pleasures of the seaside are evoked by this happy photograph from the early 1960s taken on a visit to Weston-Super-Mare.
Ladies are, from the left: Vi Roberts; Mary Roberts; Dorrie Smith; Rene Sims; Mrs E White; and Shirley Newson.
Children: Paul or David Roberts; Ann Roberts; Alison Smith; unknown; Caroline Newson; Helen Newson; Stephen Prosser; Mark Newson.

Figure 5.15 (Opposite bottom left) Pupils at the Harvest Supper.

Pupils from Madresfield C of E School sing at the 2007 Harvest Supper in Guarlford Village Hall. The children had a repertoire of bright and cheerful songs which they sang with great enthusiasm, and this set the tone for a pleasant evening which raised £678 towards the funding of a teacher's salary in the Diocese of Masasi, Tanzania.

Figure 5.14 (Opposite bottom right) The Christmas Crib, 1994.

The Reverend Canon John Green and children are sitting round the crib at the Christmas Crib Service of 1994. Elizabeth Bennett is facing and next to the crib. Andrew and Tristan Bennett are sitting on the far right. This service, usually held on Christmas Eve, has always been very popular with young children and their parents.

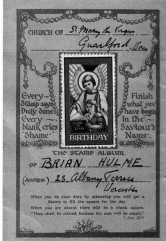

Figure 5.16 (Above)The Reverend David Nichol.

In late 1999, Guarlford, Madresfield and Newland formed a single parish and joined with the Parish of Powick to form a new Benefice. The Vicar of Powick at that time was the Reverend David Nichol, and he then took on the additional appointment of Rector of the new parish.

David is seen leading a walk around the four churches of the new Benefice, with a cross-section of parishioners from both parishes - and dogs. St Mary's Guarlford is in the background. Walking with him are his two children, Thomas and Catherine. His wife, Lynn, is the third person behind him, and to her left is Carleton Tarr, who at the time was organist and choirmaster at both Guarlford and Madresfield.

With the Millennium came new forms of worship, known as 'Common Worship', and it fell to David to introduce these across his new Benefice. In 2005, he left to take up a new post as Vicar of Holy Trinity at Malvern Link.

Figure 5.17 (Opposite left) The Remembrance Service, 2006.

Each year since the end of the First World War has seen Remembrance Services at churches throughout the country, and Guarlford is no exception. At Guarlford the service starts in the church and, after the National Anthem, the congregation makes its way out of the church and down to the war memorial where there is the familiar act of remembrance with two minutes' silence and the poppy wreath is laid. Sometimes, if a bugler can be found, 'Last Post' is sounded.

The photograph shows the parish reader, Martin Harbor, leading the procession, followed by the Rector, the Reverend Sue Irwin, and wreath bearer, Dr Peter Mayner, Chairman of Guarlford Parish Council. The congregation follows behind. In the years between the wars and for some years after the Second World War, there would have been a parade and 'march past' by the Guarlford Branch of the British Legion and other war veterans. The Guarlford Branch closed in the mid 1980s and its standard hangs in St Mary's. The collection from the service is sent to the Royal British Legion Poppy Appeal to contribute to the fund for the welfare of those service men and women and their families who are in need.

Figure 5.18 (Above) The Sponsored Cycle Ride, 1999.

On a bright, sunny day, a sponsored cycle ride in 1999 was in aid of the Worcester and Dudley Historic Churches Trust and Guarlford Church. The Trust awards grants for listed church repairs. In the group from the left are: Gill Ferris; Joan Newell; Elizabeth Tidball; Don Hill; and Pauline Cooper.

St Mary's Roof Repairs, 2007

Since 1844, St Mary's (5.19), situated in the centre of the village, has been part of the essential heritage of Guarlford, and with the passage of time the task of maintaining it in good order has become more difficult. Churches within the Diocese of Worcester, as other dioceses throughout the country, are subject to a detailed inspection by the church architects every five years. These are known as quinquennial inspections, and their purpose is to ensure that churches are kept in a good state of repair. The inspection report of 2004 advised, amongst other things, that the apex stones to the east and west gable ends of St Mary's were in poor order and should be replaced. The report also advised, on safety grounds, the re-setting and pinning of the roof coping stones of the west wall.

The main problem, of course, was how to fund the work. A specification was drawn up by the architect and the work put out to tender. The total sum required, including the architect's fees, was over £14,000. The long and difficult task of raising the money then followed and eventually sufficient funds were raised to start the work.

The stonemasons had to find matching material for the new apex stones, and then they had to be fashioned. The size and complexity of the new apex stone for the west gable may be clearly seen. The montage also shows the process of replacing the stones. To replace the east gable stone the crane had to lift it over the vestry roof.

Stainburn Taylor Ltd were the church architects for the project; and Town & Country Construction Company of Ledbury was the contractor.

Grants were gratefully received from the following:

Worcester & Dudley Historic Churches Trust:	£1,000
The National Churches Trust:	£1,000
Garfield Weston Foundation:	£1,000
Alan Evans Memorial Trust:	£1,000
Private donations:	£1,170
Elmley Foundation:	£10,000

The last to be used for repairs to both Guarlford and Madresfield Churches.

The shortfall was met from PCC funds, that is, in the main, from the congregations.

Figure 5.19 Church Roof Montage. (Don Hill & Michael Skinner).

Guarlford Weddings

Figure 5.20 (Above left) Alan Webb and Muriel Attwood.

Alan Webb and Muriel Attwood were married in 1948. Muriel was the daughter of John Attwood, who is on the bride's right.

Figure 5.22 (Opposite left) Victor Bradshaw and Florrie Price.

Victor Bradshaw and Florrie Price, Joan Bradshaw's parents, were married in 1913.

Figure 5.21 (Above right) Bill Sims and Violet Bullock.

Bill 'Doodey' Sims and Violet Bullock were married in 1938. The adult bridesmaid was Violet's cousin from Poolbrook. The little bridesmaids, Bill's nieces, were Eileen and Thelma.

Figure 5.23 (Opposite right) John Little and Cynthia Butt.

The wedding of John Little of Clevelode and Cynthia Butt took place in 1951 seen here with the Revd F Newson. The couple lived in a cottage in Clevelode which has since been demolished.

Figure 5.24 Kenneth Lawson and Molly Tombs, 1943. Molly was the niece of Bill Brewer of Grove House Farm, seen centre back.

Figure 5.25 The wedding of Charles Bladder and Phyllis Williams on the 5th June 1955.

Figure 5.26 The wedding of Charlie Williams and Doreen Clarke of New House Farm Cottages in 1958.

Figure 5.27 Reception at Guarlford Court after the wedding of Peter Harding and Katherine Pettigrew in 1972. To the right are Dorrie and Ron Smith and the Rector, Father Hartley Brown.

Figure 5.28 (Right) The wedding in 1978 of Rosemary Anne Smith and Donald McCarry, with their hunter mare 'Hyperbond' as the invited guest making an unusual picture.

Figure 5.29 (Left) Katherine (nee Deam) and Richard James leave Guarlford Church after their wedding in 2004.

Guarlford Events: Village Fetes

It is very clear from old Guarlford parish magazines going back, for example, to the years 1906 to 1911, that the village fete was one of the more important and popular events of the year. Few had the means to travel far for their leisure activities or the disposable income taken for granted today by most, but parishioners clearly knew how to enjoy themselves.

The event would start with a grand opening and Lady Beauchamp is seen performing this task in 1911 (5.30). It is a scene of some elegance, with ladies, gentlemen and children obviously dressed with considerable care and a sense of occasion far removed from the informality we are used to today. One other eye-catching feature of this photograph is the apparent spontaneity of the scene and the way Lady Beauchamp's smile is so vividly caught. There would be stalls selling local produce from the kitchen and the garden, together with needlework, arts and crafts, as in the following photographs, (5.31) and (5.32).

There would also be treasure hunts, tug-of-war, bowling for the pig, and a wide variety of races and games, as well as, almost certainly, a band. The list is endless. Fancy dress parades were popular and the cause of great activity, anticipation and quite elaborate preparation in the weeks running up to the day of the fete.

Many people owned bicycles and it is not surprising that bicycle events were also very popular and the subject of some ingenuity; for example, there were the bicycle obstacle course and bicycle musical chairs. There were bicycle races for the fastest and also for the slowest. Bicycles were numerous, popular and accessible for both work and play at this time.

Later in the evening, there was sometimes dancing on the Rectory lawn.

Figure 5.30 Countess Beauchamp opening the Village Fete in 1911, with her sons, Viscount Elmley and the Hon Hugh Lygon.

Figure 5.31 The Parish Stall at the 1911 Guarlford Fete.

Figure 5.32 Another stall at the Guarlford Fete.

The photographs of the Parish Stall, seen at the 1911 fete (5.31) and (5.32), are full of interest: as well as the elaborate stall itself, with its draped canopy, there are the tiered displays of items for sale. A sense of great satisfaction and pride in the stall is evident. Even more notable perhaps is the pride in appearance clearly demonstrated in the way everyone is dressed, especially the ladies, with their elaborate hats. There can be no doubt that the fete was an important social occasion for Guarlford.

Betty Dunn, daughter of the Revd F Newson, believes (5.33) to be a group photograph of those in fancy dress at the 1920 fete. Many adults have entered the event with great enthusiasm, it seems; cu-

riously, some of the men have taken a deal of effort to masquerade as women. It is easy to imagine the fun and hilarity the event generated. There are, however, no younger children; perhaps they had their own fancy dress parade. The gentleman on the left, in white slacks and hat, is almost certainly the Revd F Newson. Given the likely date of the picture, the considerable effort put in by those participating might suggest a sense of release after the long years of anguish and austerity brought about by the Great War.

Figure 5.33 The Fancy Dress Competition at the 1920 Guarlford Fete.

The young tycoon with cigar and wearing the bowler is Ken Rickards (5.34) and the young Guardsman in this picture is Allan Hardy. Ken's costume was meant to depict 'The Modern Youth on the Dole' for which he received First Prize for 'Class 3 Most Comical Section', which shows that there must have been many classes. The children seem to be rather fed up – perhaps the photographer is taking too long and keeping them away from the fun. Evidently, fancy dress parades were not only an important part of fetes but it is also very clear that proud parents went to some trouble to dress their children in distinctive costumes.

Most of the ladies in the background are wearing hats which are very much of the period.

A very happy scene of a fancy dress competition in the fete of 1968 (5.35), overleaf, prompts more enjoyment the more it is studied. Most of the participants have surely improvised very well. There, on the right, are Bill and Ben of black and white television fame; and on the left is the ominous though cheerful threat of student riot to come - no doubt influenced by contemporary campus unrest at the time and inspired by bearded and beret-wearing French rioters.

Then there are two delightful scallywags in ankle length football shirts and a princess complete with spectacles and tiara. The older girls are all looking very pleased with themselves, and there is just a glimpse of the head-dress of one young lady in Welsh national costume who is almost obscured by the dominant English tiara. The young cowboy is handsome in his superior outfit.

In the front row, from the left, are: John Morris; Robert Morris; Julie Morris; Timothy Nash; Andrew Thomas and Martin Thomas.

In the back row, from the left, are: Robert Prosser; unknown; Loraine Bevan; two unknown; Rosemary Young; Nicola Young and Christine Bevan.

(5.36). The Revd Hartley Brown is seen opening the fete in 1968. The other people who can be identified in the photograph are, on the left, Mr Medcalf, and behind Father Brown is Mrs Peggy Lodge. The little girl with the doll is Mrs Lodge's granddaughter, Miranda White, who currently has two daughters at Madresfield School.

The Bedford van is a typical vehicle of that era. Note also the fine pair of dining chairs, presumably brought out from the Rectory and perhaps for Father Brown and Mrs Lodge to use whilst judging the fancy dress competition.

Figure 5.34 The Children's Fancy Dress Competition at the 1935 Fete.

Figure 5.35 The Fancy Dress Parade at the 1968 Guarlford Fete.   *(Berrows Newspapers).*

Figure 5.36 Father Hartley Brown and Mrs Peggy Lodge opening the Fete in 1968.   *(Berrows Newspapers).*

Figure 5.37 Charlie Williams at the Clevelode Show.

Figure 5.38 Jackie Williams.

Horses have played a large part in the lives of Charlie Williams and his family and a sense of this is demonstrated in these photographs. He has a wonderful collection of horse brasses and other horse paraphernalia, as well as interesting documents which record the buying and selling of horses over the years.

Charlie Williams is at a Clevelode Show (5.37). It is reported that the show moved around from farm to farm in the parish. In this summer scene are, from the left: Richard Williams; David Clarke; Charlie Williams and Peter Clarke. Horses from the left are 'Archers Prince'; 'Archers Pride' and 'Lacetown Quicksilver', while barely visible at the rear is 'Judy'. Jackie Williams, daughter of Charlie, seen here (5.38) with 'Lacetown Quicksilver' at a village ride-

about in the 1980s. Ride-abouts in the 1980s were Benefice fund-raising events initiated by the Reverend David Martin. Guarlford, Madresfield and Newland each arranged events, including venues of interest and sustenance for the joint occasion. Transport was arranged between the three villages. At one ride-about this transport was provided by a fleet of vintage cars. The proceeds were shared equally between the villages for the maintenance of the respective parish churches.

Charlie is giving pony and trap rides round the village, one of the fete attractions, in 1961 (5.39), and is seen outside the bungalow at the corner of Rectory Lane patiently waiting with his young passengers for the photographer to record the moment.

Figure 5.39 Charlie Williams with his pony and trap.

Like the Jubilee years which followed in 1977 and 2002, 1953 was a year of national celebration, bringing people together in patriotic unity. At the outset of a new Elizabethan Age, there was a surge of hope and optimism, as well as relief after the Second World War, that was not to be matched twenty-five or fifty years later, albeit these were also happy occasions. Guarlford villagers played their part on all three occasions. The picture of the Guarlford fete of 1953 (5.40) leaves no doubt that this was Coronation year. The little girl on the right is clearly in patriotic mode with her dress, and she is firmly grasping her Coronation Union Jacks.

Another little girl, most probably also at the 1953 fete (5.41), is Ursula Rickards. The theme for her fancy dress was 'She wore red feathers and a hula hula skirt', based on the hit song by Guy Mitchell. The mother of Ursula and her brother Ken loved creating fancy dress costumes, and the children of the family often won prizes at local fetes, including at Guarlford. Ursula has a hula skirt with red feathers, roses in her hair and is carrying a coconut and a 'fresh fish from the sea', a model fish which she still has. Note the houses under construction in the background, which the Rickards say is Penny Close, Guarlford.

The charming picture (5.42) of four young and willing volunteers helping out with the skittles was taken at a fete in the early 1990s. They are, from the left: Rosie Fellows; Emma and Mark Twigg (twins) and Alice Huskinson. New House Farm makes a fitting backdrop. Though taken in recent years, the photograph is one which might record any Guarlford fete in the twentieth century; but it is a simple scene of completely innocent pleasure that could perhaps only have been taken at a village fete.

A scene from the dog show at the 2004 fete (5.43) brings the story of Guarlford fetes nearly up to date. It is, regrettably, a reminder, too, that this wonderful and always enjoyable village tradition enjoyed by so many over the years has now ceased, or is, at least, in abeyance. Angus McCulloch is showing his English Setter, 'Boddington', with David Masters of Hall Green officiating in the background.

Figure 5.40 (Top left) The Fancy Dress parade at the 1953 fete.

Figure 5.41 (Top right) Ursula Rickards in fancy dress.

Figure 5.42 (Bottom right) The skittle alley at the Fete in 1991.

Figure 5.43 (Bottom left) The Dog Show at the 2004 Fete.

Guarlford Events: The Silver Jubilee

The year of Her Majesty the Queen's Silver Jubilee, 1977, was an important one for Guarlford, as it was for the whole country. Celebrations were carefully planned from early in the year. The first formal meeting of the Guarlford Village Jubilee Committee took place at 7.45 pm, on 21st February, in the Rectory, with the Reverend Hartley Brown in the chair; there were twelve other members. A fascinating and detailed record of the discussions and the plans made is provided by the minute book, which is still in existence. The Secretary was Mr Michael Skinner, and his minutes are augmented by photographs of the Tidy Up Campaign, the pond clearance and the tree planting, which also marked the occasion of the Jubilee. A cheque for £75 was forwarded to the Queen's Silver Jubilee Appeal and subsequently acknowledged in the name of the Prince of Wales.

On Tuesday, 7th June, the high point of the celebrations, a Children's Jubilee Party, was held at Dripshill House, home of Major and Mrs J M Smyth. Photographs testify that it was a sunlit celebration, and entertainment included a Punch and Judy show and various activities for the children, prize-winners being presented with certificates by Major Smyth. All children received a commemorative mug. It is clear that this was a year to remember, and an example of village life at its best.

Figure 5.44 (Left) Father Hartley Brown, Cllr Major J M Smyth MBE and Cllr Mr T G Boaz MBE presenting the cheque for the Queen's Silver Jubilee Appeal to Cllr Mr J Guise and Sir John Willison.

Figure 5.45 (Opposite) The Silver Jubilee Fete Montage.

(1) The Punch and Judy Show; (2) Sara Skinner; (3) Mandy Skinner and Bernadette Kirton; (4) Mrs Smyth and Mrs Cath Lockley distributing the Jubilee Mugs; (5) The Tidy Up Group, Back Row: Cllr Major J M Smyth MBE; Mrs Helen Browning; Sir John Willison; Cllr Mr J Guise and Dr Eric Jones. Front Row: unknown; unknown; Mandy Skinner; Sian Browning; Bernadette Kirton and Jane Kirton.

Guarlford Events: The Golden Jubilee

In 2007, the Queen and Prince Philip celebrated their Diamond Wedding Anniversary. The early years of this century have already seen two royal events: 2002 was the year of the Golden Jubilee of Queen Elizabeth's reign. Although it was known that the annual fete in July would be extended to become a Jubilee Fete with extra events for the children, Guarlford Parish Council thought the parish should have a celebration on the actual Jubilee date of 4th June.

The event took the simple form of a picnic with games for adults and children, celebrations perhaps a little less elaborate than those twenty five years earlier in Guarlford. Everyone was invited to bring and share their food and this proved to be very successful, the Guarlford ladies being well known for the quality of their catering. At the kind invitation of Dr and Mrs Peter Mayner, the event was held at the charming venue of Cherry Orchard, with its beautiful outlook towards the Hills. The weather was kind and a very pleasant afternoon was enjoyed by over one hundred parishioners and guests.

During the afternoon, everyone gathered in the field, referred to as the 'Lawn' in the c.1840 Tithe Map, at Cherry Orchard for a group photograph (5.49) of the occasion with the Malvern Hills as a fitting backdrop and the flag flying high. The picture was taken from a bedroom window of Cherry Orchard.

Later, in the lengthening afternoon shadows (5.50), the younger children enjoy a game of musical chairs under the able direction of Helen Simpson of Grove House Farm.

Figure 5.46 (Opposite left) The well-stocked buffet table.

From the left: Elizabeth Tidball; Louise Warden; Val Levick; lady not identified; and Barbara Hill.

Figure 5.47 (Top right) Peter and Elizabeth Mayner.

Hosts for the occasion, Peter and Elizabeth, with the plant presented to them by the Guarlford History Group.

Figure 5.48 (Bottom right) Lunch.

One of the many groups enjoying the picnic and the sunshine in the pleasant surrounds of Cherry Orchard – Joan Bradshaw, Joan Newell and Barbara Hill are standing.

Figure 5.49 The Golden Jubilee Village Group.   (Michael Skinner).

Figure 5.50 Musical Chairs at the Golden Jubilee Picnic.   *(Noel Deam).*

Guarlford Events: The Book Launch

On 21st August, 2005, three years after Cllr Dr Eric Jones initial-ly proposed the writing of a history of the village inspired by Miss Joan Bradshaw's existing research and notes, and after many interviews, meetings and discussions by a small project group, *The Guarlford Story* was launched at Dr and Mrs Peter Mayner's home, with a large gathering of villagers and others with an interest present to celebrate the occasion. The picnic event was similar to the successful picnic to celebrate the 2002 Golden Jubilee. Again, the weather was fine, the food was excellent and the launch was attended, not least, by many old Guarlfordians returning from all parts of the country. Naturally, there was much 'catching up' to be done. The guest of honour, of course, was Miss Bradshaw herself, to whom a presentation was made. After the picnic lunch, the six authors manned the tables for a brisk session of book selling, and some books were autographed. Sales have continued ever since and should eventually fall not far short of one thousand copies.

As well as the support of the Parish Council and its dedication to the project of the prize money the village was awarded in 2002 for achieving second place in the Worcester Community Pride Com-petition, a generous donation from the Elmley Foundation and, in 2004, a substantial grant from the Local Heritage Initiative, have all made the enterprise financially sustainable. Guarlford also has a comprehensive website: *www.guarlford.org.uk*. A village archive is maintained in the village hall.

Figure 5.51 (Opposite left) Joan Bradshaw and Joan Newell.

Joan Bradshaw, who had just been presented with a copy of The Guarlford Story and a flower arrangement, with Joan Newell en-joying the afternoon with friends.

Figure 5.52 (Opposite top right) Lunch in one of the marquees.

A group are enjoying their picnic lunch. Nearest the camera, from the left: Bob Bannister, Sonia Skinner, Brian Wyndham, Pam Wyn-dham, Meriel Bennett; and facing, Barbara Hill, Joan Rumsey, Eric Jones and Siti Jones.

Figure 5.53 (Opposite bottom right) The Guarlford History Group with Joan Bradshaw.

The authors were each presented with a copy of The Guarlford Story, and afterwards this group photograph was taken with Joan Bradshaw (seated). Authors from the left are: Peter Mayner, Rose-mary McCulloch, Don Hill, Michael Skinner, Janet Lomas and Eric Jones.

Other Guarlford Events

Guarlford Parish Council initiated two projects to commemorate the Millennium. The first was a major restoration of the church pond. The restoration was very successful and resulted in a second prize of £300 in the County Council's 2002 Community Pride Competition, which the Parish Council used to support the production of *The Guarlford Story*. The second project was the planting of several trees at locations round the parish. The picture (5.54) shows the planting of a field maple at Rhydd. From the left: Dr Eric Jones; Dr Peter Mayner; Barbara Hill; Michael Huskinson; Michael Skinner; David Masters; Toby Bruce-Morgan; Janet Lomas; and, kneeling, Pauline Cooper. Also in front from the left are 'Toby', 'Cassie' and 'Juno'.

Once a month, one of the Worcestershire County Council's mobile libraries is a popular arrival in Guarlford (5.56), providing a useful service as well as a meeting point for its regular users. In earlier years the County Council distributed to Guarlford two boxes of books, probably about forty in each box. These were kept in the Village Hall, and twice a month Mrs Joan Johnson, and others before her, would open the hall and the boxes, for the local residents' benefit. From time to time, the County Council would change the boxes. The value of this service, in times before car ownership became the norm, cannot be over-stated, nor can its continuing importance as an informal meeting point. Avril Deam, (5.57), foreground, and Edna Medcalf can be seen making their selections.

In 2006, the Guarlford History Group initiated a Photographic Competition, the theme of which was 'The Guarlford Scene throughout the Four Seasons'. There was a good response, and on Sunday, 2nd September, the following year, an event was arranged in the Village Hall to display all the entries for judging (5.55). The event was combined with an exhibition of local arts and crafts, and the ladies of Guarlford WI provided refreshments. The results of the competition were:

Spring:	First	Pat Lowry;	Runner Up	Tom Vivian.
Summer:	First	Barbara Hill;	Runner Up	Tom Vivian.
Autumn:	First	Tom Vivian;	Runner Up	Tom Vivian.
Winter:	First	Keith Owen;	Runner Up	Cora Weaver.
Best on show:		Keith Owen.		

These photographs and some others selected from the competition appear throughout this book.

Figure 5.54 (Opposite top left) The Millennium Tree Planting.

Figure 5.55 (Opposite top right) The Photographic Exhibition.

Figure 5.56 (Opposite bottom right) The Mobile Library.

Figure 5.57 (Opposite bottom left) Mobile Library interior.

A Guarlford Musician: Marie Hall, International Violinist

One of the most lyrical and evocative pieces of English music, Ralph Vaughan-Williams's *The Lark Ascending*, is dedicated to a violinist who once lived in Guarlford, Marie Hall. She performed this beautiful work with Adrian Boult and the British Symphony Orchestra in London in 1921. Shortly after her birth in Newcastle in 1884, Marie's family moved to Guarlford, where they lived in one of three small cottages, now one house called 'Maywood'. Her father was Marie's first violin teacher, and the young girl who was to become an internationally celebrated violinist gave her first public performances in Church Street, Malvern, while her mother collected pennies from passers-by.

In 1895, when eleven years old, Marie became a pupil of Edward Elgar. At the age of seventeen, Marie was heard playing by the eminent Czech violinist, Jan Kubelik; this led, after further study, to an acclaimed concert debut in Prague in 1902. Some years later, by now a violinist with an international reputation, Marie's association with Elgar was renewed, and she recorded Elgar's *Violin Concerto* for HMV Gramophone Company, with the composer conducting, in 1916. Part of this recording can be heard at the Elgar Museum in Broadheath. Marie's early years in Guarlford were clearly formative ones in the making of a very accomplished musician. It is appropriate that her name is linked with two of the greatest of English romantic composers, one of them Malvern's Elgar.

Figure 5.58 Marie Hall.

A Guarlford Author: Leslie Halward, Prose Writer and Dramatist

Guarlford's own author, Leslie Halward, lived with his wife, Gwen, in a sixteenth-century Clevelode cottage they called 'O Providence', after their marriage on 29th June, 1936. The Halwards' new home delighted the writer and seems to have provided an ideal retreat after his earlier, very different Birmingham life. Signed copies of Leslie Halward's short story collection, *Tea on Sunday*, and his autobiography, *Let Me Tell You*, have been presented to the village archive, and together they provide a wonderful introduction to a writer who achieved success and recognition in the 1930s and was one of a Birmingham group of writers which included others whose names are perhaps better remembered today, such as Walter Allen and John Hampson.

There is an attractive directness about Halward's writing and he shared with many writers of the period an essential English romanticism that was removed from the iconoclasm of the self-conscious international "Modernists". As well as the short story, the wireless play, too, seems to have been a medium in which Halward was particularly at home. An article in the Malvern Gazette in October, 1950, about his eighth play for the B.B.C. described him as "... well-known to radio listeners for his human domestic and back street comedies." Leslie Halward died in 1976 and his ashes are buried in Guarlford churchyard.

Figure 5.59 Leslie and Gwen Halward.

Chapter 6

Rural Businesses and Farming

Introduction

Anyone interested in rural life and local history will be fascinated by the picture of Guarlford's rural businesses and farming in this chapter. It not only describes the businesses and farms themselves, but, in the case of farming particularly, it also describes farm equipment and practices and how both have changed. What used to be done in large measure by many hands is now done by increasingly sophisticated machines. Nothing like the farm workforce which posed so formally attired in front of a wagon load of straw in 1918 (6.48) could be found today; and the pitch forks and hay rakes have been replaced by huge combine harvesters and balers.

Agricultural and horse shows are no longer a prominent part of the rural scene, while Shire horses have all but disappeared and with them the blacksmiths' workshops which used to be such a feature of the Guarlford landscape. Local farmers today have had to diversify as traditional farming has declined, and milking herds, in particular, have gone. The marquee hire business at Grove House Farm is one example of such diversification (6.27).

Basket-making was an important local business based at Clevelode, taking advantage of the Severn and adjacent wetter farmland. The industry provided varieties of baskets for local use, as well as employment for some families. Another significant local business was that of Mr Arthur Shinn, whose prize-winning honey was well-known and appreciated locally. Today Guarlford has one successful and attractive plant nursery at Grange Farm, where earlier there were several. Village stores were to be found in Guarlford, as in every English village, ready to supply the daily needs of a population which walked rather than taking the car to shop. Pubs provided refreshment after a day's work, as, fortunately, the 'Plough and Harrow' and the 'Green Dragon' still do to this day.

Guarlford, then, still has flourishing farms and businesses, though generally different in character from those of the past.

Winter Greens by Cora Weaver.

Rural Businesses

Basket Making

The River Severn, and ditches on wetter farmland in the parish, provided conditions for growing osiers. Osier willows, or 'withies' as they were known, were cut in rotation by local families who made their living making baskets. The Hayes, the Hyde and the Little families from Clevelode were the families most dependent on basket-making. The Hayes family was the last to carry out this highly skilled trade in the parish at their workshop in Clevelode (6.1). Mrs Leonard, Mrs Paget, Mrs Nash and Mrs Arnold can be seen (6.3) at work on osier beds near the 'Homestead', during the First World War; here they are sharpening the tools, which they use to cut the withies, earning sixpence a bundle. The withies were then transported to sheds where they went through various processes before being woven to make fruit hampers for fruit pickers, baskets for linen, bread and coal, and 'putchins' for eel fishing, another local cottage industry.

Figure 6.1 (Left) Withies standing in the yard outside the Hayes workshop at Clevelode.

Figure 6.2 (Top right) Archie Jones standing beside a delivery van in the 1930s. Many tradesmen would have used locally-made baskets such as those he is carrying.

Figure 6.3 (Bottom right) Osier Pickers.   (C D Walton).
Mrs Leonard, Mrs Paget, Mrs Nash and Mrs Arnold at osier beds near The Homestead. The field was called 'Marshes' on the tithe map, but has now been drained, and there are now no longer any osiers growing there.

Village Stores

In the first half of the twentieth century, many people kept a pig and chickens and grew their own fruit and vegetables. Local tradesmen delivered many of their other supplies. These tradesmen had shops in Malvern or neighbouring villages. With horse and cart, or van or lorry, they came around with milk, coal, bread, fish (including eels caught and prepared by the local Little family), hardware, groceries, meat and many other household items.

There were shops within the parish too. The 'Tan House', next to the 'Plough and Harrow', housed a shop in the 1920s and 1930s, and older parishioners remember that it was run by 'Granny Thomas' and Mrs Ackerman, who sold a wonderful range of sweets, toys and tobacco.

At the same time, between the Wars, Mr Bosworth ran a plant nursery (2.10) in the cottage on the corner of Mill Lane. The small wooden building on the right-hand side of the cottage housed 'Barber's General Store'. Mrs Barber was a widow who sold sweets, cigarettes, and biscuits. Within a hundred yards of 'Bosworth's Nursery', near Mill Farm, there was a larger nursery called 'Marsden's Nursery', which employed eight men and women and supplied shops in Malvern and even Birmingham.

Mrs Bullock's 'Guarlford Stores' (6.4), used to stand on the edge of the common in front of the cottage where Mrs Bullock lived, at 110 Guarlford Road near the 'Green Dragon' public house. Mrs Bullock ran the shop between the Wars with her daughter, Vi Sims. It was described as a 'one-stop-shop' selling everything from fireworks to faggots supplied by the butcher from Hanley Swan. Customers would stand in the porch and ring the shop doorbell. Mrs Bullock would come down the path from her cottage and let herself into the shop via the back door, and then admit the customer into the shop to serve them. The building was pulled down some time in the 1970s, though its sign still exists.

Figure 6.4 Mrs Bullock's Guarlford Stores, 110 Guarlford Road.

Sale of Farm Produce

Before the Second World War, farmers of the parish had to play a larger part in the marketing of their produce than they do today. New House Farm, Guarlford Court, Fowler's Farm, Priestfields, Rose Farm and Honeypots Farm had milk rounds in and around Malvern, competing with one another and others outside the parish for custom. Some farmers had their own shops. During and after the Second World War, Teddy Waters of Heriots Farm and his family had a shop called 'Heriots Farm Dairy' in St Johns, Worcester, and a dairy round which delivered to doorsteps, originally by horse and float, and later by Ford 8 van, on the way to the shop where they also sold home grown fruit and vegetables.

The Lanes from Woodbridge Farm had a 'high class florist and fruiterer's shop' on Holyrood Terrace in Great Malvern. They used to grow vegetables and flowers at Sherrard's Green, and Mr Lane would go round the farms with a horse and cart to buy eggs, butter and dressed chickens to sell in the shop. The shop is seen (6.5) in the 1930s, where many types of vegetable, including cauliflowers, are on display. Edwin Lane, who still lives at Woodbridge Farm, remembers his father telling him that during the Malvern Festivals, George Bernard Shaw often used to stay at the Foley Arms Hotel and would call in to the shop to buy peaches, which were grown by Edwin's uncle in his peach house at Blackmore Gardens in Hanley Swan. The Lane family were told that on one occasion Edward Elgar was with him.

Figure 6.5 The Lane's Shop, Holyrood Terrace, Great Malvern.

Figure 6.6 Guarlford Court was one of many farms in the village which had a milk delivery round between the Wars. Mr Absalom Bradshaw, Joan Bradshaw's grandfather, is driving the float around 1900 with his elder son, also Absalom, known as 'Abbie'. Milk was ladled from the old-fashioned churn into householders' own jugs.

Guarlford's Pubs

This (6.7) is an early photograph of the 'Plough and Harrow', when it was only licensed as a beer and cider house. There was no bar at that time, but the Landlord positioned himself by the doorway leading into the inner area and refilled mugs as required. After the Second World War, Dick and Pam Capstick renovated the pub and obtained a full licence. The owner of the three-wheeled bike in the photograph has not been identified. Older residents of the parish remember that several local characters rode tricycles, before and after the Second World War, including Ray Cole, the blacksmith's son, and the last Countess Beauchamp.

Figure 6.7 (Right) The 'Plough and Harrow'.

Figure 6.8 (Opposite top left) The 'Plough and Harrow', 2007. The current tenants are Juliet Tyndall and Michael Weir.

Figure 6.9 (Opposite right) The 'Green Dragon' and possibly the landlord whose name, William Powell is above the door.

Figure 6.10 (Opposite bottom left) The Croome Hunt Meet at the 'Green Dragon', in the middle of the twentieth century.

Businesses Keeping Horse and Vehicles on the Road

Over the twentieth century, motorised vehicles gradually re-placed the horse, which had been essential to many rural businesses and local people who could afford to use them in the fields, the workplace and for transport. So the blacksmiths' shops had plenty of work shoeing horses, as well as making and repairing many of the tools of trade for farmers and other local businesses.

There were three blacksmiths working in Guarlford between the two World Wars. Mark Young and his father opened 'Old Elm Forge' in 1926-27 located in a brick building, with timber beams held together with wooden pegs. It still stands today next to 74 Guarlford Road, (6.12).

Harry Wellings ran his smithy from Little Heriots, in Clevelode Lane, and also travelled by bicycle to work two or three days a week at the blacksmith's shop at Home Farm, Madresfield, where he shod Lord Beauchamp's famous grey Shires. Harry worked as a blacksmith until the 1940s, when he retired. His premises were pulled down, and the A J Gammond Ltd premises now stand on the site. Mr Raymond Cole, whose smithy was in Chance Lane, also had a wheelwright business near the two twisted pear trees on the common.

The bills from Young's and Cole's (6.11) show examples of what these skilled craftsmen produced and supplied. Felloes and strakes were parts of wheels. Felloes were the wooden pieces which, when nailed together, end on end, formed the round shape of the wheel. A strake was the tyre of the wheel. Before the practice of bonding continuous metal tyres onto wheels, short lengths of tyre were used. These were put on hot and would cover a felloe joint and end at the centre of the felloe. They were then nailed and cooled. It was a method used before a technique was discovered to make a continuous tyre. It meant that no measuring was required and this system was still in use until the 1950s, because farmers believed it gave better grip. The wheelwrights disagreed, so for a while wagons had both a continuous bonded tyre next to a straked tyre, making the outside of the wheels very thick. A continuous tyre gives a far better and stronger wheel.

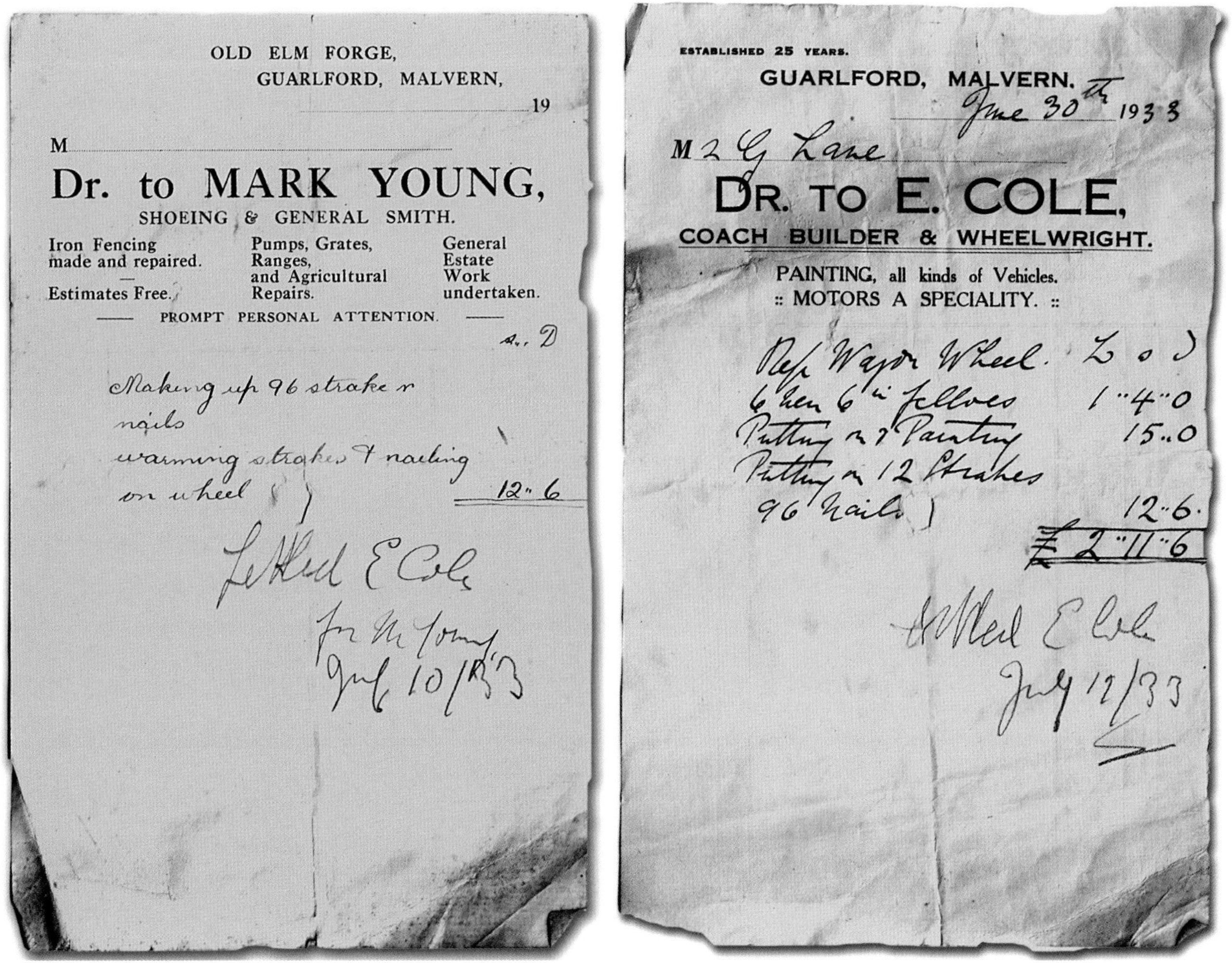

OLD ELM FORGE,
GUARLFORD, MALVERN,
———————————19

M ————————————

Dr. to MARK YOUNG,

SHOEING & GENERAL SMITH.

| Iron Fencing made and repaired. | Pumps, Grates, Ranges, and Agricultural | General Estate Work |
| Estimates Free. | Repairs. | undertaken. |

—— PROMPT PERSONAL ATTENTION. ——

s. D

Making up 96 strake r
nails
warming strakes & nailing
on wheel }   12. 6

Le Hred E Cole
for M Young
Jul 10/33

ESTABLISHED 25 YEARS.

GUARLFORD, MALVERN.
June 30th 1933

M 2 G Lane

DR. TO E. COLE,

COACH BUILDER & WHEELWRIGHT.

PAINTING, all kinds of Vehicles.
:: MOTORS A SPECIALITY. ::

Rep Wagon Wheel.   £ o d
6 hen 6 in felloes   1 . 4 . 0
Putting on & Painting   15 . 0
Putting on 12 Strakes
96 nails }   12 . 6.
                      £ 2 . 11 . 6

Hred E Cole
July 12/33

Figure 6.11 Bills from Mark Young, the blacksmith, and Raymond Cole, the coach builder and wheelwright, 1933.

In addition to his blacksmith business, Mr Cole was a coach-builder and wheelwright. He built carts and wagons for farmers and tradesmen, and older locals remember the finished vehicles painted in bright colours standing outside, near the junction of Chance Lane with Guarlford Road, to be admired by passers-by until collected by their owners.

Later, the site of Cole's blacksmith shop was taken over by 'Woodwards Coaches', and finally the premises were occupied by 'Miles Transport' whose business appears in the photograph in figure 6.15 around 1970. The fuel from the pump shown in the photograph was not for public sale. When Miles Transport closed, the buildings were pulled down, and the land became part of the common.

After the Second World War, many local people who owned a vehicle could buy petrol from the Bladders, who had a pump on the side of the road at Fowler's Farm. Humphrey Bladder remembers that they had to return the petrol coupons to the fuel suppliers if they wanted a fuel delivery.

Humphrey, who is attending the pump in the photograph in figure 6.14, which was taken around 1951, remembers that they had two tobacco tins in the shed by the pump, one for petrol coupons, and one for cash. Nothing was ever locked up, and nothing was ever stolen!

Figure 6.12 (Above) Young's Smithy, c.2006. (Rosemary McCulloch).

Figure 6.13 (Top left) Cole's Wheelwright, c.2006. (Rosemary McCulloch).

Figure 6.14 (Right) Fowler's Farm Petrol Pump, c.1951.

Figure 6.15 (Bottom left) Miles Transport, c.1970. The vehicles include a Daimler Dart and a Minivan.

Arthur Cecil Shinn and his Beekeeping Business

Arthur Cecil Shinn was born in Guarlford in 1902. His mother had always been interested in bees, but Arthur himself did not take up keeping bees until the 1920s, when, so the story goes, a swarm landed in his garden. He built up a business, which flourished until the 1950s or so, but also continued to keep bees and produce honey until his death in 1983.

As described in Chapter One, when the name of Mr Arthur Shinn is mentioned to people who lived in the village from the 1930s onwards, they always remember his bees and the wonderful honey produced at the pretty black and white cottage on the Guarlford Road. Customers came from all over the area, including Dame Barbara Cartland. Dame Barbara would come to buy Arthur Shinn's honey whenever she visited her mother, Polly Cartland, who lived at Littlewood House, Poolbrook, from 1931 to 1976.

Arthur won many prizes in local and county shows, some of which are shown on the following pages, as a producer and as a small-holder. He had hives not only in his own garden in Guarlford but also took them all over the country. For example, he left hives on a relative's farm at Great Barrington in the Cotswolds at the time when the clover was in blossom for clover honey; for Welsh heather honey, he would leave hives in Radnor.

Arthur would get up very early to shut up his bees in their special 'National Hive', and with them well closed up, he would drive them to their new homes for a few weeks. Bees are still valued by fruit growers, and today most of the bush orchards of Herefordshire have hives, often borrowed during spring from beekeepers to aid pollination of the blossom.

Some of Mr Shinn's products are shown in Figure 6.18. Royal Jelly is also a product of beekeeping, and is produced by worker bees to keep the queen bee well-nourished and fertile. Royal Jelly, taken as a food supplement, is reputed to have powerful immune-boosting and revitalizing properties.

Figure 6.16 (Left) Mr Arthur Shinn with his friend, Mr Lissimore, on the right, who is holding the 'puffer'.

Figure 6.17 (Above) Mr Shinn in the mid 1930s with prizes won for his honey and honey products.

Figure 6.18 A younger Mr Shinn displays some of his products, honey in tall jars, honeycomb and beeswax.

Figure 6.19 Mr Shinn's Certificate of Merit for honey, won at the Three Counties Show in 1931, which was held in Hereford. The venue of the show used to rotate around the three counties until 1957, when the permanent showground site at Blackmore Cross was acquired.

Recent Businesses

Tan House Plants

In 1984, Malcolm Russell began selling home grown plants from his home, the Tan House, where he lived with his mother Mrs Mary Bruce. 'Tan House Plants' next door to the 'Plough and Harrow' public house, gradually developed, until Malcolm was selling a wide range of bedding plants, shrubs and roses. Apart from local customers, Malcolm's growing collection of unusual herbaceous perennials, his knowledge of the needs of the plants he sold, and his extremely reasonable prices were attracting an ever-increasing number of customers from further afield.

In 1995, Pauline Jones joined the expanding business, and a couple of years later after Mary became ill, Sue Edwards joined the team, and Tan House Plants went from strength to strength; but sadly the business closed after Malcolm's death in 2001.

Figure 6.20 is a photograph of Malcolm (right) and Sue Edwards with Ken Pountain who worked at the nursery, outside the Tan House. Figure 6.21 is a photograph of Malcolm on a stand of plants and bulbs for sale at a Madresfield Court Gardens 'Autumn Colours Open Day'.

Figure 6.20 Malcolm (right) and Sue Edwards with Ken Pountain. (Pauline Jones).

Figure 6.21 Malcolm Russell with his plants at Madresfield Court Gardens.   *(Pauline Jones).*

Grange Farm Nursery

After the Second World War, Joan Newell and Joan Bradshaw farmed at Grange Farm, where they kept horses and milked cows. In 1973, they started Grange Farm Nursery, converting the farm buildings to accommodate an office and sheds for the new enterprise. In 1975, Carol Nicholls began working at the nursery on Saturdays, and after attending Pershore College of Horticulture, bought the nursery in 1980. Unlike Malcolm's nursery, Carol's is supplied by outside sources. Carol has won awards and medals from the Royal Horticultural Society at the 'Malvern Spring Garden Show', and there is always a varied display, well appreciated by the many gardeners who visit Grange Farm Nurseries.

Figure 6.22 (Above) The Nursery Shop, 2007.   *(Janet Lomas).*

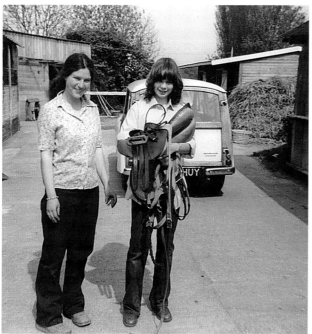

Figure 6.23 (Above) Carol Tozer (now Nicholls) with Sara Skinner in May, 1979, when horses were still stabled at Grange Farm.

Figure 6.24 (Top right) An aerial view of Grange Farm before the Nursery was created.

Figure 6.25 (Bottom right) The Nursery entrance. (Angus McCulloch).

A J Gammond; Classic Marquees

Every farmer in Guarlford and beyond feels very fortunate indeed to have the facility of 'Gammonds' on its doorstep. The original civil engineering and land drainage business, 'Gammond and McKay', was set up in 1964 by John Gammond and a colleague, on the site of Harry Wellings's blacksmith shop at Little Heriots.

As the government encouraged drainage and improvement of agricultural land in the 1960s and 1970s, the business flourished; and, in 1974, John Gammond bought out Mr McKay. John's two sons subsequently joined him in the business, 'A J Gammond Ltd'. As demand for land drainage fell, 'Gammonds' diversified. They manufactured and retailed agricultural machinery and parts, including Renault tractors and spares. They now undertake land and road excavation and retail water pipes and drainage equipment. It was Gammonds who removed the silt from the Church Pond in the village during the pond's restoration in 2001. Furthermore, they stock a wide range of parts and fittings, and have come to the rescue of many a local farmer on numerous occasions, providing an excellent 'family firm' service to facilitate a repair to the baler, or other implement in use, before the weather breaks!

One of the newest businesses in the parish, 'Classic Marquees', is run from Grove House Farm, by farmers Michael and Helen Simpson, who have a variety of marquees for hire for all occasions.

Time moves on, and with the arrival of personal computers, working from home has increased, and now many small businesses are run from homes in the parish. Planning regulation has a tight control on the scenic approach to Malvern through the village and parish, affecting the degree of change of use of buildings, and outwardly there are few signs of these new enterprises. The parish has retained its agricultural character, and farming remains the most conspicuous business activity, although it now employs very few people.

Figure 6.26 (Above) The 'A J Gammond Ltd' premises, Clevelode Lane.   (Janet Lomas).

Figure 6.27 (Right) A 'Classic Marquee'.   (Helen Simpson).

Farming

Farmyards and Livestock

Figure 6.28 Sarah Brewer of Grove House Farm, in the 1930s.

Most farms before the 1970s would have had livestock as well as crops. Laying hens, usually seen scratching around the farmyard, were often the responsibility of the farmer's wife.

Figure 6.29 Pigs at White House Farm.

Pig sties at White House Farm, where Mr Billy Bott farmed. The pigs would be fed largely on household scraps and other waste.

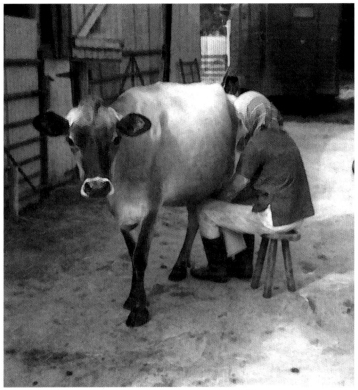

Figure 6.30 Joan Newell, Grange Farm.

Joan Newell hand milks a Jersey cow, which is standing qui-etly to be milked in the yard at Grange Farm.

Figure 6.31 Mrs Bott, White House Farm.

Geoffrey Bott's mother is bottle-feeding lambs. A lamb whose mother had insufficient milk or who had died was often bottle-fed. Where a surrogate mother is not available, bottle-feeding still takes place on sheep farms.

Figure 6.32 (Above) Julia Guest.

Alan Webb farmed at Portocks End in the 1950s, and this photograph shows his daughter, Julia Guest, with a huge sow and her litter. The sow is an old-fashioned breed, 'Large Black'.

Figure 6.33 (Above) Patrick Nugent with a Hereford Bull at Pixham Farm, 1956. Pat and his brothers also farmed at Falconers Farm.

Figure 6.34. (Opposite) Geoffrey Bott and his dog Rex.

This photograph was taken on land near Deblins Green rented for grazing by Geoffrey Bott from White House Farm. Here he is with his sheepdog, Rex, and ewes and lambs in springtime. Before the current practice of ear-tagging livestock for identification purposes, an initial or mark would be stamped, or more recently sprayed onto sheep, in this case, the letter 'B' for Bott.

The photographic study, seen on the opposite page and on the cover, is by C D Walton, the well known Barnard's Green photographer; it shows Henry Bladder of Fowler's Farm, striking a deal.

Henry was Humphrey Bladder's father and Derrick Bladder's grandfather. The cart on the right of the photograph is a manure cart, which would be used to carry manure from the farmyard to the field, where it would be tipped out onto the field in small heaps, and spread by hand with a fork. This was the usual way of supplying nutrients to crops grown in the parish until after the Second World War, when inorganic fertilisers became more widely available.

Figure 6.35 The Deal.   *(C D Walton).*

Agricultural Shows

Between the Wars, most families in the parish grew their own vegetables, and possibly kept bees, a pig or hens, and many with commoners' rights would have had sheep. They would have tried to be as self-sufficient as possible, as wages were very low. Many of them would have taken great pride in their cottage gardens and their produce, and would have the opportunity to display and compete at Madresfield Show. Each year the Craft Tent was full of delicious honey, jams, chutneys, cakes and other produce and crafts. These were always called 'Cottagers' classes, to distinguish them from professional producers' entries, and they continued until the Show's demise in the late 1990s.

The first Madresfield Show was held at Home Farm, Madresfield, in 1894. In the mid 'thirties, the Madresfield Agricultural Society, who ran the show, had a disagreement with the Lygon family, and a new venue had to be found. For three years, the Show was held at Mr Bullock's Mill Farm, Guarlford, in the field behind the Box House on the Guarlford Road.

The Show was not held during the War years, but after the Second World War, Lady Beauchamp asked Robert Bartleet of Pickersleigh Court and later of Cherry Orchard, to re-start the Show at its original venue, where Madresfield Court and the hills formed a magnificent backdrop, and he agreed. His original 1934 drawing of the show was reproduced on the annual programme and also on the Centenary Commemorative mugs of 1994.

There was another show in the parish, which was mainly a horse show. The Clevelode Show was started in about 1970 by Mike and Pat Mayhew who lived at Severnlands, just over the Clevelode crossroads where the show was held for the first few years, after which it moved regularly to a new venue. One venue was Bush Farm at Callow End, and another was a field off the Hanley Road. The show continued until the 1980s, when Malvern Hills Riding Club ran it for a few years before it ceased.

Figure 6.36 The bull class being judged at Madresfield Show in 1936, when the show was held at Mill Farm.

Harvest

Before mechanisation, corn was cut with a reaping 'hook and crook'. This first stage of harvest took place before the grain was dry; the cut corn was gathered up into sheaves and each was secured by winding a few long stems of corn around the sheaf and securing with a knot. The sheaves were then stacked in rows in the field and left to finish ripening and to dry. Later, the horse-drawn reaper-binder was introduced which cut the corn and tied it automatically into sheaves. After the Second World War, tractors pulled reaper-binders instead of horses. Older locals who worked on the land around the middle of the twentieth century remember harvesting with reaper-binders.

When the sheaves and grain had dried, the sheaves were then pitched by hand onto a wagon and taken to the rickyard or threshing barn where they were built into stacks or stored until the arrival of the threshing machine on its tour of the farms over winter. The sheaves would be fed into the steam or tractor engine-driven threshing machine, which carried out the process of separating the grain from the straw. The straw was drawn into bundles called 'boltings', later to be stored in the rick.

Some farms had early 'balers' in the 1950s which compacted the straw into large bales held in shape by wires.

By the 1960s, the 'combine harvester' had arrived; 'combines', as they became known, cut the corn when the grain was dry, and carried out the whole process of separating grain from the straw, and dropping the straw into rows behind the combine which was later baled. The very first combines were trailer combines towed by tractors, but before long they were self-propelled. At first they had very narrow five-foot cutters whereas the headers on modern combines are up to thirty feet wide. Combines separated the grain into sacks on the combine; when the sacks were full, they were tied and dropped on the ground. It would take two men together to lift the two hundredweight (cwt) sacks onto the trailer, which would take them back to the farmyard. The next development allowed grain to be augered directly into a trailer, which was driven alongside the combine. A facility to store grain in a tank on the combine soon followed. The tank of grain, when full, was then emptied into a grain trailer.

Figure 6.37 A horse-drawn reaper-binder, led by Charlie Williams who is demonstrating the process.

Figure 6.38 (Left) Combine harvester, c.1960.

This photograph is thought to have been taken around 1960. It shows Geoffrey Bott driving his combine harvester and Gordon Beauchamp helping, as Joe Yapp stands beside the ex-army Bedford lorry. The lorry had to drive alongside the moving combine as grain poured out of the chute. Modern combines can store grain in a tank, to give a trailer time to cart the corn to the farm.

Figure 6.39 (Right) Wheat is harvested by Mike Simpson's John Deere combine harvester in Autumn 2007. (Angus McCulloch).

Figure 6.40 (Left) The grain is emptied into a trailer. (Peter Mayner)

Figure 6.41 (Right) A grain trailer containing wheat being carted from the field back to the farm, where it may need to be dried before storage and sale, or before being used to feed stock.   (Angus McCulloch).

Haymaking

Hay is made in summer to provide winter feed for cattle, sheep and horses. The quality of hay depends to this day on the weather during the process of haymaking. Early summer grass is mown, spread out to dry in the sun, and is turned again and again until it is dry.

Until modernisation after the Second World War, the grass was mown by the horse-drawn mower. When dry, until the advent of balers, the hay was pushed up to the elevator by a 'sweep', which was on the front of a tractor. The loose hay was then either carried by the elevator or lifted or 'pitched' onto the hay rick in the field, or on a wagon to be drawn to the rickyard. A horse-drawn 'monkey and gib' or an elevator was often used to take hay to the top of the rick. Finally, the rick would be thatched to prevent rain penetrating; there were several farm workers who would undertake much of the rick thatching in the parish, which required great skill. Local regions had their own style and shape of rick building and thatching.

Tractors replaced horses, and, over time, the design and performance of the mower and other implements improved; but it was the arrival of the baler, which revolutionised the process of haymaking. The baler can compact hay, to make the process of transporting it and storing it more efficient. The first bales were larger than the traditional rectangular bales, and were held together by wire, but wire was soon replaced by baling twine. Bales could be 'pitched' or thrown up onto trailers or stacks; they could be stacked neatly, and could be carried easily to feed stock.

Back in the farmyard, as farmers took up the new technology, the hay ricks made from loose hay were replaced by stacks of bales. Over the years, balers have been designed to produce bales, which are large and round, or large and rectangular, and machines rather than men are required to move them. Not only does the modern machinery remove the extremely hard work, but once the hay is baled, the process of getting the baled crop under cover is faster, and the valuable winter feed is at less risk of damage from wet weather.

Phyl Bedington is seen standing (6.42) on the right in front of the wagon of hay with her good friend, Molly Tombs, at the beginning of the Second World War. Molly was Bill Brewer's niece, and it is thought that the man standing at the top of the elevator on the load is Bill Brewer, as the photograph was taken on his farm, Grove House Farm. Molly married Mr Lawson during the War and Phyl married Owen Bayliss soon after the War. The elevator was used to take hay to the top of the load. Two foals run alongside the wagon, which is probably drawn by their dams.

Figure 6.42 A Hay Wagon at Grove House Farm, c.1939.

Figure 6.44 (Below) Mowing.

Charlie Williams mowing grass at Guarlford Court, soon after the Second World War.

Figure 6.43 (Above) Horse-drawn mower.

Bill Morris riding on Billy Bott's mower, later used by Edward Jenkins, who moved to White House Farm to work for Mr Billy Bott in 1942. This mower was used by Edward to mow hay for other farmers on their farms in the parish.

Figure 6.45 (Above) Ron Smith pushing up hay with a tractor and sweep.

Figure 6.46 (Right) Hay rick at Guarlford Court Farm, c.1950.

Figure 6.48 (Below) Severn End, 1918.

This formal photograph was taken in 1918 at Severn End on the Lechmere estate at Hanley Castle. The farm workforce and household staff pose in front of a wagon load of straw with pitch forks and hay rakes, which may have been to celebrate the completion of harvest.

Figure 6.47 (Above) Guarlford Court Farm, 1960s.

A traditional mixed farm in the 1960s: Edward Jenkins remembers building the stack of straw, and filling the Dutch barn with hay and straw bales, the main stock of food and bedding for winter. The farm buildings were, from bottom left of the photo, clockwise, cart shed, the sheds where pigs were kept with manure heaps outside, calf housing, milking shed and cow bar forming three sides of the fold yard, and granary above stables near the straw stack (recently converted to a house).

Figure 6.49 (Above) Andrew Medcalf 'teds' the hay (in the foreground) at New House Farm before Daniel Bladder bales it.

Figure 6.50 (Top right) Daniel Bladder lifts two big rectangular bales and stacks them in the Dutch barn at New House Farm.

Figure 6.51 (Bottom right) Daniel Bladder stacks big rectangular bales at New House Farm, with his JCB 'Loadall' which would do the job in a fraction of the time of that taken by the elevator on the right of the picture. A man would place small bales on the elevator, which would take them to the top of the stack, where another man would have to carry each bale to its place on the top layer of the stack, as the stack grew. Many farmers still use small bales today, and some still use elevators, although there are now mechanical grabs which do the job, reducing manpower and time.

Horses at Work and Play

Horses were still the main source of power on farms until after the Second World War; those who worked on farms continued to keep horses either for some tasks or for leisure or both until the last working horses died when they were replaced altogether by modern machinery.

Opposite is Bill Morris (6.52), who worked for Mr Billy Bott, driving two horses that are pulling a cartload of spoil, removed from the farm pond in around 1940. Edward Jenkins, who worked at White House Farm from 1942, remembers being told that four hundred cartloads of spoil were removed from the pond, and that one of the horses collapsed and died during the process.

Until mains water arrived and the field tanks were fed by mains supply, a pond near the farm buildings would have been essential to water livestock, especially dairy cows giving milk. The tranquil scene of cattle by the pond is at White House Farm (6.53), where Mr Billy Bott milked Dairy Shorthorn cows; the rick yard and big barn are in the background.

Figure 6.52 Bill Morris at White House Farm, c.1940.

Figure 6.53 White House Farm Pond.

Figure 6.55 (Below) Joan Bradshaw.

Joan Bradshaw and her nephew, John, taken in the 1950s.

Figure 6.54 (Above) Bill Brewer.

Mr Bill Brewer, who farmed at Grove House Farm until the 1950s, with a two-wheeled corn wagon that would have been used to bring sheaves of corn in from the field.

Figure 6.57 (Below) Edward Jenkins.

Edward Jenkins recalls the special occasion when this photo was taken at Moat Farm, Sherrard's Green, around 1950. Edward wore a top hat to drive the dray, specially adapted for the day, with red carpet and benches, to carry members of the Women's Institute around the gardens at Madresfield Court. The dray, (drays had four wheels), was drawn by a horse called 'Short'.

Figure 6.56 (Above) The Croome Pony Club.

Bill Medcalf of New House Farm is on the far right.

Farms Today

Dripshill Farm

Figure 6.58 Richard Burford with John, Ben and Hannae of Drip-shill Farm.   (Janet Lomas).

Figure 6.59 Dripshill Farm.   (Janet Lomas).
The farm now offers Bed and Breakfast accommodation.

Fowler's Farm

Figure 6.60 (Top left) Humphrey Bladder, with Dan and Kelly at Fowler's Farm. Humphrey and Dan have a suckler herd of cattle and have diversified into agricultural contracting. (Janet Lomas).

Figure 6.61 (Top right) Fowler's Farm.   (Janet Lomas).

Figure 6.62 (Bottom Left) Dan driving a Renault tractor pulling a 'Claas' big baler at New House Farm.   (Janet Lomas).

Woodbridge Farm

Woodbridge Farm has been farmed by the Lane family since 1762 when John Lane became a tenant; he later bought the property in 1775.

Recently, most of the land was sold to Mr Chris Burton, who now farms it. However, Edwin Lane retained the farmhouse and eight acres.

Figure 6.63 (Above left) Woodbridge Farm House, 2007. (Janet Lomas).

Figure 6.64 (Above right) Edwin Lane and his sister, Margaret Omar, 2007.   (Janet Lomas).

Figure 6.65 (Above) Mr Burton, who farms part of Woodbridge Farm, 'rows up' hay before baling at Cherry Orchard, 2007. (Peter Mayner).

Figure 6.66 (Top right) Mr Burton and Rio Mayner, Dr Peter Mayner's grandson, take a break during baling at Cherry Orchard. (Peter Mayner).

Figure 6.67 (Bottom right) Rio stands beside a round bale. (Peter Mayner).

New House Farm

Figure 6.68 Andrew Medcalf.   (Janet Lomas).

Andrew Medcalf 'rowing up' his hay crop, with New House Farm buildings in the background.

Figure 6.69 The Medcalf Family, 2007.   (Janet Lomas).

From left to right, back row: Sarah Medcalf, Elizabeth Fellows, David Fellows, Rosie Fellows, Linda Medcalf; front row: Sue Fellows, Edna Medcalf, Andrew Medcalf and the dogs 'Wafer' and 'Meg'.

Figure 6.70 New House Farm viewed from Rectory Lane, 2007.   *(Janet Lomas).*

White House Farm

Figure 6.71 Geoffrey and Jacky Bott, with their son and daughter, Edward and Claire.

Figure 6.72 Edward Bott baling on the common.   (Janet Lomas).

Figure 6.73 White House Farm, c.1930, and the insert in 2007.

Grove House Farm

Figure 6.74 Grove House Farm, 2007.   (Janet Lomas).

Figure 6.75 The Simpson Family, 2007.   (Janet Lomas).

Grove House Farm is farmed by Michael and Helen Simpson.

Left to right: Michael, Jennifer, Helen and Andrew Simpson with their dogs 'Jasper' and 'Clara'.

Figure 6.76 (Left) Ewe and lambs, Spring 2007.

Michael Simpson is with his ewe and her six lambs, all of which survived. It is rare for a ewe to give birth to sextuplets, and unusual for them to have survived.

Figure 6.77 (Above). Andrew Simpson 'tedding' hay, spinning it out to dry in the sun.   (Janet Lomas).

Chapter 7

The Impact of War

Introduction

The two World Wars of the twentieth century had considerable impact on the lives of the people of Guarlford, as can be seen in the photographs of local men and women wearing the various uniforms of the armed forces, as well the uniforms of those who served on the home front. In their impact on Guarlford, the upheavals of the two World Wars were experienced in Guarlford much as they were everywhere else in the country. Villagers left their homes and were sent to distant places, men were wounded and taken prisoner, and several died. Cdr F J Ratcliff RN saw active service in both wars. Frank Williams was awarded the Military Medal in the First World War and, in the Second, Charles Bladder was 'Mentioned in Despatches'. A memorial in St Mary's honours those who fell in 1914 – 1918 and 1939 – 1945.

At home, the wars were a constant presence in daily life both through the concern for family members whose exact whereabouts and safety were unknown and through the preparations of the Home Guard, while the Land Army, too, brought the Second World War into people's lives. Armistice Day, 1942, saw an impressive parade of local men in the uniform of the Home Guard. Mass evacuation of city children across the nation led to Guarlford and its school providing a new home for a number of children, some of whom still recall this dramatic change in their young lives.

Later conflicts have also had an impact on Guarlford residents, albeit it is individuals who have been affected, not the whole community. Dr Peter Mayner served in the 'Canberra' as Senior Surgeon during the Falklands campaign of 1982 in the South Atlantic. More recently, Dan Besgrove has experienced the dangers of present-day Iraq and Afghanistan.

Remembrance Day every November brings sombre reflection on these conflicts, with two Commonwealth war graves nearby.

Personalities

Corporal Frank Williams MM (1) was awarded the Military Medal (MM) in 1918 while serving in France with the Worcestershire Regiment. He was badly wounded and left with five bullet scars down his back. After the war, he left the army with the rank of Sergeant to pursue a career in the Metropolitan Police.

The MM was instituted in 1916 as an award to non-commissioned ranks for gallantry in the face of the enemy. Junior officers and Warrant Officers received the Military Cross (MC). In 1993, the MM was discontinued and the MC became available to all ranks of all services for exemplary gallantry on land in the presence of the enemy.

George Bedington (2) is seen during the First World War with his wife, Clara, and baby daughter, Phyllis (later Phyl Bayliss).

John H Tandy, 11th Essex Regiment, (3) died on active service in 1918 and is buried near Ypres. His father was sexton at St Mary's, and John attended Guarlford School. In the Second World War his son, Ken, served in the Herefordshire Regiment, while his other son, Bill, served in the RAF.

Victor Bradshaw, (4) father of Joan, wore the uniform of a Special Constable during the Second World War, and was also a church-warden for many years.

Corporal Frank W Brush, (5) whose parents lived at Rhydd, served in the Corps of Military Police in the Second World War. He was awarded a certificate of merit for his devotion to duty during the invasion of France. His father, a postman from Hanley Swan, lost an arm in the First World War.

The duties of the Military Police include the vitally important management of the huge volumes of military traffic generated by armies on the move.

John Bedington (6) joined the Royal Navy in the Second World War, qualifying as a gunner on Defensively Equipped Merchant Ships, known as 'DEMS', and served in them throughout the war. War-time documents retained by John show that he was taken on as a deck-hand to disguise his RN status should his ship enter a neutral port. This happened at least twice: at New York, before the United States entered the war, and Lisbon. His anti-typhus documents show he spent Christmas, 1944, in Port Said, Egypt. He spent some time in the RN hospital at Liverpool and had further training in Calcutta in 1945 before discharge in 1946.

Colin Bradshaw (7) is seated front row centre with his RAF bomber crew. Having trained in Canada as a fighter pilot, Colin was re-assigned to bombers and flew at least 37 sorties in Lancasters. Note the survival whistles on each crewman's collar.

Figure 7.1 Some of Guarlford's Military Personalities.

The Home Guard

Mention 'Home Guard' and many will think of 'Dad's Army' and Captain Mainwaring with his platoon at Walmington-on-Sea. In May, 1940, the reality was far more serious. German forces were sweeping towards the Channel, culminating in the evacuation of the British Expeditionary Force from Dunkirk between the 27th May and the 4th June, and the threat of an imminent invasion of the United Kingdom was very real. In particular, there was the threat of enemy paratroops intent on the capture or destruction of vital points throughout the country ranging from telephone exchanges to power stations and railway junctions.

On the 14th May, Anthony Eden announced over the radio the formation of the 'Local Defence Volunteers' (LDV). They had no organisation, staff, funds or proper weapons; listeners were simply instructed to give in their names at the local police station. Within 24 hours, 250,000 men had registered their names. By the end of June, the total numbers exceeded 1,400,000. In July, 1940, Winston Churchill changed the name to 'Home Guard' and initiated proper military training, a command structure and supply of uniforms, arms and equipment. The main duties of the Home Guard were to keep watch and ward; to inform the police in the event of any paratroop landings and to repel such landings to their utmost, until the arrival of reinforcements. Men, in addition to their normal work, would be expected to do two or three nights' duty each week, as well as evening and weekend training. The Home Guard also became a key contributor to civil defence, liaising with the police and assisting the fire fighters. However, by 1943, when the threat of invasion receded, the Home Guard lost much of its sense of purpose and on the 3rd December, 1944, it was stood down. Some 1206 had been killed on duty or died from wounds and 557 sustained serious injuries.

Men from Guarlford served in the Malvern Division Company of the Home Guard. Some mustered with their section at the Morgan Works in Pickersleigh Road. Others seem to have met at Madresfield Court. The Morgan Works had been requisitioned by Sir Alan Cobham's 'Flight Refuelling' venture; he was housed at Pickersleigh Court during the war.

A comprehensive account of the Worcestershire Home Guard can be found in Mick Wilks's *The Defence of Worcestershire in World War II*, Logaston Press, 2007.

Figure 7.2 The Armistice Parade, 1942. From the left are the British Legion members, nine members of the Home Guard followed by cadets and members of the ARP or Observer Corps. Cadets were affiliated to Home Guard units for training purposes.
Known individuals are: 2nd left, Captain Chester; 3rd, William Brush; 4th, Fred Brush; 9th, Wallace Bladder; 10th, Dick Gowen; 13th, Keith Chester; 17th, Alan Webb; 18th, Ken Peek. (As recalled by Keith Chester and others).

Figure 7.3 D Section, 3 Platoon, Malvern Division Company, Home Guard, outside the Madresfield Court stable block.

Front rank: centre, Earl Beauchamp and 1st from the right is John Tomkins. Second rank: 2nd left is John Sexton; 5th left is Dick Gowen. Rear rank: 2nd right is Alan Webb and 3rd right is John Bedington. The photograph was probably taken in Spring 1941, the platoon having just received their new uniforms.

Figure 7.4 Keith Chester in Home Guard uniform with his brother Paul.

Keith joined the Home Guard late 1941. His memories of those times include the following:

"We had regular morning parades at the Morgan works, next to Sir Alan Cobham's Flight Refuelling Co, a pioneer in refuelling aircraft in flight. I'm blowed if I can remember much of what we did, except drill and unarmed combat. Night guard duties provided further excitement when we guarded Malvern from the top of the Link church tower. Between solo star-gazing we could sleep on iron bedsteads but there was a flourishing card school going all night. Transport for me was by my brother Paul's motorcycle until he joined the Royal Engineers (finishing up as adjutant in the Madras Sappers & Miners in India) then in the back of Alan Webb's van as he passed from Portocks End, also picking up a wonderful old timer, Dick Gowen, from a cottage near Little Heriots. Sometimes we also collected Mr Wall from Grove House Farm. Farmers and farm workers attended parades and exercises when they could be spared from their more important day jobs.

We were nearly useful once. Paul and I were turned out at dead of night in early 1942 when an Me 110 crashed about where the Malvern Showground is now. By the time we got there, the crew of two had been collected so we went back to bed. We did not forget to take with us our shared rifle. No bullets of course – so much safer that way.

We did get some shooting practice, with army rifles, at the West Malvern range and also with .22 rifles at an indoor range beneath the GPO at the top of Church Street." Subsequently, the range became the headquarters of the Malvern Conservative Association.

Evacuees

Guarlford had its fair share of evacuees during the Second World War, mainly from the Midlands. The School Log records that on 20th November, 1940, twenty-three children from Selly Park School joined the village school. The following excerpts from their reminiscences give a small insight into their lives at that time.

Mr A R Rose from Solihull wrote:

"It was like a different world to the kids from Birmingham, being evacuated right out in the country at Guarlford; all those animals and fields everywhere, and the rich smells of the countryside. We were fortunate in being evacuated to Guarlford Rectory in the care of the Reverend and Mrs F Newson where we were very well looked after, and very well fed in spite of rationing. I shall never forget those wonderful Sunday dinners, and the blackberry and apple puddings; it was a marvel of good housekeeping and good cooking.

How Mrs Newson managed to cope with ten evacuees, as well as her own family, for several years is beyond me, but we were grateful for it. It wasn't just the task of getting meals for sixteen people every day but all the other little problems: sickness, relatives wanting to visit etc. They ought to give medals for this sort of thing."

He also wrote:

"The Rectory was a fascinating and interesting place to live, with lots of people coming and going there. All the kids were given their own little plot in the garden to dig and plant; I don't think we were too keen on gardening though."

Mrs Anne Franklin from Worcester wrote:

"My sister Janet and I were evacuated to a cottage up from Medcalf's farm. We attended Guarlford School and I seem to remember it was a large classroom divided by a curtain and Miss Cole and Miss Gosling were our teachers. There was a third classroom which was uninhabitable due to a large hole in the floor. The cottage was lit by oil lamps, the bathroom was a shed and water was carried from the pump and heated on an oil stove. The loo was down the garden. The school had visits from injured American forces stationed at Blackmore Camp, who always arrived with candies and gum for us. I remember a ditch on the right hand-side before the gate to the church and can recall seeing an upturned jeep there – they missed the corner too! I used to walk every day to the Medcalf farm for a billycan of milk and also walk to Barnard's Green to collect 'refilled' batteries for the wireless."

Reg Bevan recalled being evacuated from Selly Park School kitted out with his name label and a cardboard box with its string 'shoulder strap' containing his respirator, or gas mask as it was more

Figure 7.5 Mrs Frances Newson with a family friend and children during the Second World War. Mrs Newson is in the centre with friend to her right. The two blonde boys are believed to be two of her sons, Richard and Michael. The other children are evacuees. Miss Vi Rose is second left in the front row.

commonly known. He stayed for over five years at Woodside, a smallholding in Blakes Lane owned by Mr and Mrs Raines.

"I wore proper shoes to school but in the evenings and weekends I wore either 'wellies' or wooden soled clogs." He remembered the generosity of the American forces and whenever he had the chance he and two or three other lads would slip over to the American Army Hospital at Blackmore to scrounge cookies, candy, gum

or whatever they could. He remembered the crashed 'Beaufighter' incident and also taking time off school with the other children, complete with tiny union flags, to see the King, Queen and entourage speed through the village on their way to an appointment he knew not where. After the war, the Raines emigrated to Canada.

Mr Ken Brampton says he was evacuated from Birmingham with his brother and sister to the Long family in a cottage on the Rhydd road near the 'Plough and Harrow' but now demolished. He says he was not happy and did not stay long in Guarlford.

The Listening Post

Figure 7.6 Internal and external views of the Listening Post in Rectory Lane as it was in the Second World War; note the sten guns propped against the wall by the door on the top insert. It was used to track the movement of enemy aircraft by monitoring their radio traffic. For a while, after the war, the building became the home of Ernest and Violet Clarke and their family.   (Dstl, MOD, Crown Copyright).

An Episode in Iraq

Dan Besgrove, from Guarlford, joined the scientific staff of RSRE in 1983 and transferred to the private sector five years ago. Below, he graphically describes a recent technical visit to Iraq.

"I have worked at various overseas locations throughout my career, most recently in Iraq, installing and testing some equipment for one of our customers.

During a recent trip there, our inbound Hercules C130 flight to Basra Air Station was aborted due to the airfield being mortared as we were on final approach – however, we managed to land safely. The next ten days consisted of a hectic schedule of long working hours, little sleep and multiple helicopter flights, mostly in the middle of the night. I found the most challenging part of the trip to be working at 'The Shatt Al Arab Hotel' in Basra City in temperatures of over 120 degrees. The heat and conditions there made working very hard (we ran out of fresh water one day) and as my body had not had time to adjust to the temperature, I found sleeping virtually impossible. In addition to the heat, the troops occupying the hotel had to deal with regular missile and mortar attacks. A few weeks before I arrived, a Lynx helicopter was shot down 500 yards from my sleeping quarters, causing the first female fatality of the operation.

Having seen first-hand the working conditions and dangers, I have nothing but admiration for our service personnel and am proud that I have been able to play a small part in supporting their operations. This continues the family tradition of either serving in the military or providing services in support of it. The photograph shows me on the roof of a UK base in Basra where I spent much of my time working through the night (with just some local bats for company)."

Figure 7.7 Dan Besgrove in Basra.

SS Canberra and the Falklands Conflict

On the 2nd April, 1982, Argentina invaded the Falkland Islands. Two days later, the Peninsular and Oriental Steam Navigation Company liner, 'SS Canberra', was requisitioned to serve as a troopship in the task force hastily formed to re-take the islands. For the next 98 days, the lives of the ship's company were dramatically changed, including that of Dr Peter Mayner of Guarlford, Senior Surgeon, and his medical staff.

By 7th April, 'Canberra' was at Southampton undergoing major alterations to equip her for her new role. This included the provision of a major hospital facility. Three days later, with 2,500 troops on board, she set sail with the task force for the Falklands. On board, Peter and his medical staff worked closely with Surgeon Captain Wilkes RN and his medical contingent to prepare for the forthcoming conflict. Peter founded the 'Canberra Medical Society'.

In the early hours of the 21st May, the task force entered 'Falklands Sound'. The commandos and paratroops from 'Canberra' and the other vessels then disembarked to engage the Argentine forces and establish a bridgehead. The first attack by a single 'Pucara' aircraft came at 08.50 hrs. This was followed by waves of attacking aircraft at half-hourly intervals for most of the day. Several bombs straddled the 'Canberra', which responded with machine guns and shoulder-fired missiles, but she was not hit. The frigates and destroyers of the Royal Navy took the brunt of the attack. Several were badly damaged. HMS 'Ardent' was sunk and her survivors were transferred to

'Canberra'. Throughout the battle, casualties from the other ships and the shore landings were also transferred to her, including Argentine soldiers. That evening 'Canberra' slipped away to rendezvous with the 'Queen Elizabeth II' in the relative safety of South Georgia. It was too dangerous for her to linger in San Carlos water. On the 2nd June, she returned with the Scots and Welsh Guards; these disembarked and 'Canberra' left safely the next day, there being no air attacks. Whilst there, Peter took his medical team to visit the field hospital set up by the RM Commando Medical Squadron in an old sheep slaughterhouse. Surgeon Cdr Rick Jolly wrote: "With a characteristic and instinctive generosity, Peter very kindly left a case of beer for the lads. Never were a few mouthfuls of cold Australian beer more gratefully accepted."

On 14th June, the Argentine forces on the Falklands surrendered.

Dr Peter Mayner wrote: "After the surrender, we took 4,144 Argentinian prisoners of war (POWs) back to Puerto Madryn, Argentina. This was a Welsh-speaking community on a natural harbour with a half mile jetty out into deep water, built for the iron ore carriers. On embarkation, the POWs were in poor health and it was necessary to screen them for illness. We appealed for their medical personnel to identify themselves, but only one medical orderly came forward to help us. It was fortunate that the trip was less than twenty four hours. Many of the young conscripts were so grateful for the warmth of the ship and the first hot meal for weeks."

Figure 7.8 'SS Canberra' at anchor off Ascension Island, taken from a landing craft full of marines returning after an exercise ashore.

On the 24th June, with a full complement of Marines from 40, 42 and 45 Commando on board, 'Canberra' set sail for home, arriving at Southampton on 11th July to a tumultuous welcome.

The 'Canberra' medical staff, including the P&O team, had received 172 casualties, of whom eighty-two were British and ninety were Argentine. Many were seriously wounded but none died – a record of which they were all justly proud.

Figure 7.9 The P&O Medical Team.

When 'Canberra' was requisitioned, Peter Mayner, a RAFVR officer, and his entire medical team volunteered for the Falklands conflict.

Left to right:
Angela Devine, Nursing Officer; Jack Last, Dispenser, retired WO1 RAMC and ex Far East POW (Friend of fellow POW, the late Major Monty Smyth); Dr Peter Mayner, Senior Surgeon; Rosemary Elsdon MBE, Nursing Officer; Dr Susan West, Assistant Surgeon.

In memory of the men of Guarlford who fell in the two World Wars.

1914-1918

John Eyton-Lloyd	Royal Flying Corps	1917
Herbert Little	Somerset Light Infantry	1917
Thomas Panting	Royal Field Artillery	1917
Philip Panting	Duke of Edinburgh's Wiltshire Regiment	1918
Frank Scrivens	Worcestershire Regiment	1917
John Tandy	Essex Regiment	1918
James Walker	Herefordshire Regiment	1917

1939 – 1945

Dennis Jackson	Worcestershire Regiment	1944
John Woolley	Royal Air Force	1941

They shall not grow old, as we who are left grow old:
Age shall not weary them, nor the years condemn.
At the going down of the sun and in the morning
We will remember them.

Figure 7.10 Dr Peter Mayner lays the poppy wreath with the Reverend Sue Irwin and Martin Harbor on Remembrance Sunday, 2006.

Figure 7.11 Armistice Sunday c.1942. Second left is believed to be Captain Chester and third right is the Revd F Newson. The lady with banner and the girls in uniform are believed to be from the Girls Life Brigade (later to combine with the Girls Guildry to become the Girls Brigade). Just visible in the rear ranks can be seen members of the British Legion, Home Guard and local Cadets.

Chapter 8

Neighbourhood Groups

Introduction

In this final chapter of *The Guarlford Scene* the photographs show the present-day residents of the village. Inevitably perhaps, there are some gaps, but the majority of the village's inhabitants of all ages are pictured in 2007 sitting or standing in their corner of Guarlford or the village hall, plant nursery or pub. This amounts to a unique record for the future. It is probably true to say that it is only rarely that such a collection as this is created. The village is its people. They are seen here in portrait groups, and as groups they are rather different in character from the snapshots which make up the majority of the photographs in *The Guarlford Scene*: they are more deliberate and were taken for the purposes of the present book. Even those of us who live in Guarlford would almost certainly not recognise all of our individual neighbours if we were to meet them by chance, such is modern life and the more dispersed way we live when compared with our forebears; but at least we and our readers can see who we all are by consulting these group photographs! Some photographs have a slightly more formal aspect than others, and even have a hint of the annual school photograph, but they have in common an evident pleasure in the occasion, as neighbours are brought together for this experience and its reinforcement of a sense of shared local identity as Guarlfordians. Village pride matters and so does our sense of ourselves as neighbours.

Taken together, the photographs in this chapter provide what amounts to a 'map' of the village from Guarlford Road to Chance Lane to Bamford Close to Penny Lane and Close, together with Rhydd and Clevelode, the latter two small population centres each separated by a short distance from the heart of the village, which might be said to be St Mary's Church. The other group portraits show the Parish Council, the Parochial Church Council, church members, the Women's Institute, and the owner and staff of Grange Farm Nursery. Not least, we see the 'Village Elders' who regularly share memories and good cheer in the setting of Guarlford's quite ancient 'Plough and Harrow' pub. They, like everyone in the photographs collected here, have been brought together for this publication. In this way, as in the accompanying narrative, we both celebrate Guarlford and add our various contributions to its story.

Rectory Lane by Colin Lettice.

The Bamford Close and Rectory Lane Neighbourhood Group

Back Row

Michael Skinner; Colin Lettice; Tony Stock; Simon Wyndham; Cyril Thomas; Graeme Cox; Dan Besgrove.

Middle Row

Don Hill; Bob Bannister; Ray Jones; Brian Wyndham; Sheila Cox; Rosie Huskinson; Lynn Jones; Pauline Bannister;

Eric Jones; Michael Huskinson.

Front Row

Wendy Ashcroft; Dorothy Thomas; Doreen Lloyd-Jones; Mandy Besgrove; Barbara Hill; Pam Wyndham; Siti Jones; Sonia Skinner.

Bamford Close, a small group of eleven timber-framed houses, was completed in 1972; originally it was called 'Cherry Orchard Close', but the similarity in name with Mr Bartleet's, now Dr Mayner's, 'Cherry Orchard' house a little further up Rectory Lane caused some confusion to the postal services. As a result the Parish Council changed the name to its present one, based on some research by the Chairman, Major Monty Smyth, which showed that there used to be some land in the vicinity called 'Bamford's Piece'.

Nevertheless, even with this less attractive name, Bamford Close has proved to be a popular place to live, as shown by the infrequent changes of ownership over the last thirty-six years. The photograph shows the residents of Bamford Close, together with some families from adjacent houses in Rectory Lane. Unlike earlier times, when most parishioners worked on the land, the occupations of those shown here cover a wide range; amongst those present are, either working or retired, an accountant, an academic, a medical practitioner, several scientists, a military officer, a solicitor and the former captain of a very large oil tanker.

These residents of Bamford Close, although they might be regarded as relative newcomers, play a significant role in village life; the group includes three parish councillors, the clerk, two members of the Village Hall Committee, a St Mary's Churchwarden, several members of the WI and four members of the History Group.

Figure 8.1 The Bamford Close Neighbourhood Group, 2007. (Peter Mayner).

The Chance Lane Neighbourhood Group

Back Row

Bob and Rose Cartwright; Angus McCulloch; Brendan Thorne; Don Thomas; Matthew Thorne; Sarah Morris; Shelagh Thorne; Nigel Morris; Michael Thorne.

Middle Row

Bill Longmore; Graham Byford; Mary Thomas; Rosemary McCulloch.

Front Row

Joseph Loveridge (aged 11); his cousin James Longmore (aged 13) and 'Boddington' the English Setter.

Chance Lane runs along the boundary of the Civil Parish but is well within the Ecclesiastical Parish. The photograph was taken on the common in front of two very old pear trees with twisted trunks, which once grew in the garden of a cottage, standing with several others in this area, now common land. Two 'Moorcroft' variety Perry pear trees were planted nearby in 2006. Also to be seen on this site in the first half of the twentieth century would have been the wagons and carts made and repaired by Mr Cole the wheelwright (of the Chance Lane Smithy). Later followed Woodwards Coaches and Garage, complete with its petrol pump, and then Miles Transport.

Don and Mary Thomas built their Chance Lane house in 1954, and Mary, with her brother John, supplied many memories for *The Guarlford Story*; they are descendants of the Little family of Clevelode.

For over sixteen years, Graham Byford delivered post to the nearby Guarlford Road Estate, and the link continues as Nigel and Sarah Morris also work for the Post Office.

The Thorne and Cartwright families have long been resident in Chance Lane, home for Brendan and Matthew Thorne since birth.

Bill Longmore is a retired farmer who moved to the lane with his family some years ago, and Angus and Rosemary McCulloch are members of the Guarlford History Group.

Figure 8.2 The Chance Lane Neighbourhood Group, 2007.   *(Helen Jones).*

The Clevelode Neighbourhood Group

From Left to Right

Chris Bond; Peter and Shirley Quy; John, Emma and baby Eathen Powell; Chris Roberts and Jane Hadley-Roberts; Lucy Allum;

Ken Jeynes (kneeling); Jo Thomson; Alan Rogers; Richard Allum; Jean Shaw; Helen Rogers; John Shaw.

Clevelode has for a long time been an important place in its own right. Judging by Roman pottery found in the vicinity, some of it being identified as the distinctive Severn Valley Ware from the Malvern kilns, there was a thriving community here. Since shards of this ware have been found in many places in the country there must also have been a quay at Clevelode for the distribution of the pottery.

A chapel, certainly there before 1250, stood on what is still called 'Chapel Hill' where a few traces can be found (shown on the Ordnance Survey map). William Bennet was Chaplain there after the Dissolution, when in Edward VI's reign an inventory for Clevelode Chapel included "One chalice of sylver and gylte, one lytle belle, vestment of yellow sylke". In 1595, the Rectory of Clevelode was annexed to that of Madresfield, the two places being small and unable to support two priests and the churches lying "but a mile from each other". Clevelode's little chapel soon fell into disuse, and by 1674 it finally collapsed.

Clevelode was also a place where the river could be forded in early times. Before the Norman Conquest it was the chief crossing. At four to six feet deep it was shallower than either Pixham or Rhydd, the latter being six to twelve feet deep before it was further deepened in the nineteenth century. It was quite a busy place; in 1296, twenty-nine people were liable for tax.

In Medieval times Clevelode was the principal quay for Malvern. The Severn was an important trade route, and in the fifteenth century the stone for the re-building of the Priory tower was floated down the river from Highley in the north of the county and unloaded at Clevelode.

In the nineteenth and twentieth centuries, the people of Clevelode were mainly occupied in fishing (for salmon and eels) and basket-making. Villagers also still remember swimming from the 'beach' and jetty as children, as well as fishing and taking out punts and rowing boats.

Figure 8.3 The Clevelode Neighbourhood Group, 2007.   *(Matthew Hadley).*

The Rector and Church Wardens of St Mary's, Guarlford

From Left to Right

Dr Peter Mayner; Pauline Cooper, Church Warden; Martin Harbor, Reader;

the Reverend Sue Irwin, Rector; Don Hill, Church Warden.

This photograph was taken on Remembrance Sunday, November 12th, 2006. Dr Peter Mayner, Chairman of the Parish Council, laid the wreath of poppies at the War Memorial on behalf of the people of the village.

This was the first Remembrance Service taken in the parish by the Reverend Sue Irwin. After some years working in Stock Exchange Investment in the City of London, Sue trained for the Ministry where she found herself a pioneer of various changes in the Church of England.

In 1979, she was amongst the first women to be ordained Deaconess directly from Theological College, and she served in parishes in Birmingham and in Surrey. The first women Deacons, including Sue, were ordained in 1987, and she served as a Deacon in Surrey and near Oxford.

Seven years later, in 1994, the first women priests were ordained, Sue among them. She then served as a priest in parishes in Oxfordshire, Berkshire and Buckinghamshire.

In 2006, history was made once again when Sue became the first female Rector of Guarlford. Sue cares for the Benefice of Powick and Guarlford and Madresfield with Newland. The Benefice consists of the Parish of Powick with the church of St Peter and the daughter church of St James at Callow End, and the Parish of Guarlford and Madresfield with Newland (with our two churches dedicated to St Mary the Virgin). Sue also visits regularly the Church of England Schools in the villages of Madresfield, Powick and Callow End. She is assisted across the Benefice by a group of four Readers including Martin Harbor of this parish. (Readers can conduct certain services but cannot administer the Eucharist.)

Figure 8.4 The Rector and Churchwardens, 2006.   (Michael Skinner).

Part of St Mary's Congregation

From Left to Right

Judith Knott; Thora Jolley; Lynn Hartshorn (nee Bunch), visiting from America; Edna Medcalf; Sylvia Bunch; Pauline Jones;

Don Hill, Churchwarden; Cherry Gray; the Reverend Biddi Kings, Associate Priest; Barbara Hill; Alan Tummey;

Ken Watts; Margaret Tummey; Penny Witcomb and her daughter, Francesca Witcomb.

There is a Service in St Mary's, Guarlford, on most Sundays between 9.30 and 10.30 am, and here are some of the congregation with the Associate Priest, the Reverend Biddi Kings, after a service in the summer of 2007.

Biddi joined the Benefice ministry team in December 2006, serving in the four churches. She was ordained as a Non Stipendiary Minister (NSM), which means that she receives no payment for her work as a priest, and Biddi said, "Some people find this difficult to understand because being a minister in the Church of England demands a great deal of time and commitment, but for me whatever time and energy I can give is a way of saying 'thank you' to God."

The training and qualifications of a priest such as Biddi are exactly the same as for those who take on the responsibility of paid ministry as a vicar or rector, but at the time when this photograph was taken Biddi was a full-time priest who worked part-time in the Benefice. Her duties included leading and preaching at the various regular services in church, occasional services such as baptisms, weddings and funerals, and helping to meet the pastoral needs of all the people in the parish, whether or not they were regular churchgoers.

Of her calling Biddi said, "For me it is a joy that I relish, great fun and truly a privilege to lead worship and to share fellowship with all the different members of the community I meet."

Through family circumstances, Biddi relinquished her licence to serve as an Associate Priest to the Benefice at the end of 2007.

Figure 8.5 St Mary's Congregation, 2007.

The Grange Farm Nursery

From Left to Right
Mark Baddeley; Cath Lockley; Carol and Rollin Nicholls, Owners.

Carol Nicholls, the owner of Grange Farm Nursery, has always been interested in horticulture, and in 1975, at the age of fifteen, she came to ask 'the two Joans', Miss Bradshaw and Miss Newell, if they needed a 'Saturday Girl'. After her 'A' Levels at Ledbury Grammar School, Carol attended Pershore College of Horticulture, where she was given the award for Top Student of her year. She continued to work at Grange Farm and eventually became a partner in the business, finally buying the Nursery in 1980 when the two Joans retired. Carol is always ready to give advice about plants and has a keen interest in the horticulture industry as a whole.

Rollin, Carol's husband (and childhood sweetheart), has now joined her in the business, having himself been awarded an HND in Horticulture at Pershore as a mature student.

Carol has always had great support from her family and friends, as well as her dedicated staff. Mark Baddeley has worked for Carol for twenty-five years, and Cath Lockley has been involved with the Nursery since the time of the two Joans. Cath, a true Guarlfordian, was born and bred in Guarlford and still lives in the centre of the village. At first she used to take over the care of the Nursery when the two Joans had their regular Tuesdays off and now works there almost full-time.

Another employee for many years is Lois Speedy, Rollin's sister, so this is very much a local family business. Many will agree that there is something different about Grange Farm Nursery; indeed, for many people living outside the village, the Nursery often comes to mind first when Guarlford is mentioned.

Grange Farm Nursery is open every day except Christmas Day, 9 am to 5.30 pm in the Summer (5 pm in the Winter), and from 10 am to 5 pm on Sundays. Customers find not only excellent plants in the attractive setting of the original farm buildings, but also the expertise and knowledge of a true horticulturist in its owner, Carol.

Figure 8.6 The Grange Farm Nursery, February 2008.   *(Michael Skinner).*

The Guarlford Parish Council and Officers

Back Row

Janet Lomas, Tree Warden; Cllr Michael Huskinson, Vice-Chairman; Cllr Michael Simpson; Cllr Dr Eric Jones; Cllr Andrew Medcalf; Mike Partridge, Public Path Warden.

Front Row

Michael Skinner, Clerk; Cllr Dr Peter Mayner, Chairman; Cllr Barbara Hill; Cllr Jane Hadley-Roberts.

The Parish Council was created in 1894; initially the parish was quite large as it extended into Great Malvern as far as Pickersleigh Road. However, in 1933, after protracted negotiations with the Malvern Council, the parish was reduced to its present size and the number of councillors reduced from nine to the current seven. The present councillors were all elected uncontested in April, 2007, and represent a good cross-section of the community.

The Chairman, Cllr Dr Peter Mayner, a semi-retired medical practitioner, has lived in the parish for over fifty years; the Vice-Chairman, Cllr Mr Michael Huskinson, is a solicitor and an Honorary Canon of Worcester Cathedral; Cllr Mrs Jane Hadley-Roberts runs a bed and breakfast establishment at Clevelode; Cllr Mrs Barbara Hill is a Server at St Mary's; Cllr Dr Eric Jones is a retired academic; Cllr Andrew Medcalf farms New House Farm and Cllr Michael Simpson farms Grove House Farm.

The Council also has three officers, the Clerk, Michael Skinner, the Tree Warden, Mrs Janet Lomas, and the Public Path Warden, Mike Partridge. Michael was invited to become clerk some twenty-seven years ago when the Council was unable to persuade anybody else in the parish to take up the position. Mrs Janet Lomas is a conservation advisor for the Herefordshire Farming Wildlife Advisory Group, who, with her husband, Edward, farms Home Farm, Madresfield. Janet's roles are to advise the Council on the maintenance of trees and wildlife in the parish and also on the maintenance of Church Pond. Mike Partridge is a retired scientist who has recently joined the Council as the Public Paths Warden; his job is to monitor the state of the footpaths within the parish and to liaise with both the landowners and the County Council to ensure that they are kept in good repair.

Figure 8.7 The Guarlford Parish Council, 2007.   *(Harriet Baldwin).*

The Guarlford Road Neighbourhood Group

Back Row

Gill Crisp; Mike Partridge; Muriel Partridge; Kay Burns; David Kershaw; Richard Percy; Joan Ballinger; Warren Ballinger; Chris Burns; Sue Jones; Judith Ashcroft; Mark Jones; David Ashcroft; Irena Percy.

Front Row

Judy Kershaw and Derrick Bladder, with (standing) Natalie Jones and Jasmine Jones.

All these neighbours have lived in Guarlford Road for twenty years, some for thirty years or more!

Derrick Bladder came to live at The Glen, Rhydd Road, when he was two years old; his father, Cooper, moved from Redditch to work for Derrick's Grandfather Henry Bladder at Fowler's Farm. Judy Kershaw's grandparents, Mr and Mrs Dick Gowen, lived in Clevelode Lane, and Judy remembers coming from Malvern Wells as a child to visit them.

Mark and Sue Jones took over the 'Green Dragon' in 1987 and since then have extended the pub, building up a good reputation for the excellent food served in their large conservatory dining room.

The photograph was taken in front of beautiful Laburnum House, and this part of the Guarlford Road stands close to some of the earliest settlements which grew into modern-day Malvern. From the sixteenth century onwards, many thatched timber-framed cottages stood alongside the road, of which some survivals remain near the 'Green Dragon'.

Also nearby, at the junction with Hall Green, was the village pond, known as 'The Fladder', which once was large but is now merely a hollow, although the floods of 2007 showed something of what it was like many years ago. This pond was used between the two World Wars by the many animals that grazed on the common.

Figure 8.8 The Guarlford Road Neighbourhood Group, 2007.   *(Graeme Crisp).*

The Parochial Church Council

Some of the members of Guarlford and Madresfield with Newland PCC, Guarlford Village Hall, July 2007.

Back Row
Chris Bennett, Churchwarden Madresfield; Peter Hughes, PCC Secretary.

Middle Row
Allan Tummey; Don Hill, Churchwarden Guarlford; Pauline Cooper, Churchwarden Guarlford; Sam Watson; Eddie Gover;

Val Levick, Churchwarden Madresfield.

Front Row
Barbara Hill, Server; the Reverend Sue Irwin; David Kuun, Treasurer; Martin Harbor, Reader.

Parochial Church Councils were first given legal status in 1919, and each PCC is responsible for the financial affairs of the Church and the care and maintenance of the church fabric and its contents. Before 1919, these matters were the legal responsibility of the incumbent and the churchwardens, and the members of congregations had little say in the running of the church except in electing the churchwardens. The PCC also has a voice in the forms of Service used by the church and may make representations to the Bishop on matters affecting the welfare of the parish.

The office of churchwarden has existed since the thirteenth century, and by the fifteenth century churchwardens were elected by the adult parishioners.

There are usually two churchwardens in each parish, but since the two ecclesiastical parishes of Guarlford and Madresfield with Newland merged in 1999 to form a single parish with two parish churches, there have been four churchwardens on the PCC.

Figure 8.9 The Parochial Church Council, 2007.   *(Michael Skinner).*

The Penny Lane and Penny Close Neighbourhood Group

Back Row
Dennis Hewins; Keith Owen; Michael Brown; Jenny Brown; the Reverend Edward Williams; David Jarrett.

Front Row
Cath Lockley with granddaughter Amie; Dot Hewins; Mrs Vi Clarke; Rosemary Williams; Mary Jarrett.

When this photograph was taken, Mrs Clarke was the oldest resident of the village. She was married to Ernie Clarke, of New House Farm cottages, and because of lack of housing after the Second World War the couple asked the Medcalf family if they could live in the abandoned brickbuilt Radio Listening Post in Rectory Lane. They moved in with their young family and stayed there happily for a few years, before moving in the 1950s to one of the newly built houses in Penny Close. Mrs Clarke died in September 2007.

Dot Hewins has cared for the Village Hall for many years and often arranges flowers in the parish Church.

Dennis Hewins has lived within the ecclesiastical parish since he was two months old, when his family moved to 'Denbrean' in Mill Lane, a house named after the two brothers, Brian, the elder, and Dennis. He was the Parish Footpath Officer for some years.

The newer Penny Lane houses were built in 1971, and many of the families have lived there for much of that time, among them Cath Lockley, who is descended from the Sims and Waters families, inhabitants of the village for many generations.

The Reverend Edward Williams is a retired Baptist Minister, and he and his wife Rosemary served in India for ten years in the 1960s with the Baptist Missionary Society. Edward taught Physics at Serampore College, near Calcutta. Rosemary's father, Reg Green, was a grandson of the Pantings (see Guarlford Families) and wrote an interesting account of life in the first part of the twentieth century not only in Guarlford but also in Dudley, where he was born.

Mike and Jenny Brown have lived in the village since 1979, while retired teachers David and Mary Jarrett are comparative newcomers, having arrived in 2005.

Figure 8.10 The Penny Lane and Penny Close Neighbourhood Group.   *(Mark Lockley).*

The Rhydd Neighbourhood Group

Left to Right

Pauline Cooper; Jill Bramson; William Smith; Jacqui Smith; Ted Tompkins; Rachel Smith; Sadie Tompkins; Pat Smith; Kelly Seward; Ian Seward; Robyn Seward; Eric Seward; Pat Hessel and 'Jamie' the Dalmatian; Paul Prosser; Stephen Curril; Russell Faraday; Jeanette Faraday; Charmaine Heath; Terry Heath; Rosie Prosser; Lucy Prosser with baby Abbe and 'Dillon' the dog.

At the junction of the B4211 to Malvern with the B4424 to Callow End lies the settlement of Rhydd, established near the crossing of the River Severn. The word 'rhydd' means 'ford', and the Rhydd Crossing was part of an important ancient saltway route from Droitwich to the Malvern Hills and beyond into Herefordshire.

According to the notes of the late Joan Bradshaw, in the Iron Age a fort was established on Dripshill to guard the river ford, which was the nearest crossing place between the 'camps' on the Cotswold escarpment and Bredon Hill and the large encampments at the Herefordshire Beacon and Midsummer Hill.

Writing his *Views from the Hills* in 1963 'Coriander' described the Anglo-Saxon tribe of the Hwicce who came up the River Severn in the seventh century to Rhydd and cleared land between there and Poolbrook to make their settlement at the foot of the Malvern Hills.

In his unpublished account *Severn Fords and Ferries in Worcestershire* (1982), H W Gwilliam says that in the nineteenth century coals and bricks transported on the River Severn were unloaded at Clevelode and Rhydd, and a ferry is said to have operated across the river until 1914.

Rhydd Court was built in 1805 by the Lechmere family, and from 1906 to 1914 local communicants were occasionally invited to early morning communion services in the chapel. The house was used as a Red Cross hospital in the First World War and as a centre for evacuees in the Second. It became a school in the 1950s, Cliffey House, which closed in 2004.

Figure 8.11 The Rhydd Neighbourhood Group, 2007.   (Michael Skinner).

The 'Village Elders'

Left to Right
John Gammond; Derrick Bladder; Peter Mayner; David Brickell.

On many Saturday mornings a group of gentlemen, nicknamed 'The Village Elders', can be found deep in conversation with Dr Peter Mayner in the 'Plough and Harrow', often recalling memories of Guarlford. Some of the group are shown in the photograph opposite.

John Gammond was born in Madresfield and, after spending his early years in Whitbourne, he moved to Guarlford when his parents bought Little Heriots. In the 1960s John used his experience in the Ministry of Agriculture to set up an agricultural engineering business nearby, situated most appropriately on the site of Harry Wellings's Smithy in Clevelode Lane and which he now runs with his two sons.

Derrick Bladder has lived in Guarlford since 1924, and as his family lived at 'The Glen' on Rhydd Road, he has known the 'Plough and Harrow' for years and seen many changes in the building. When the pub received a full licence and was no longer just a 'beer and cider house' after the Second World War, Derrick was the first customer to be served with a glass of whisky. He often met there Leslie Halward, the writer, from Clevelode Lane, who describes the 'Plough and Harrow' thus: "From time to time I visit the little pub nearby, where an oil-lamp hangs from the low beamed ceiling, and drink a pint or two of beer drawn straight from the wood, perhaps play darts with the farm-hands, labourers, and road-menders who frequent the place." *Let Me Tell You* p.288.

David Brickell is the fourth generation of the bakery family in Callow End, which also served the people of Guarlford. The business began in 1856, and, as a project, David has restored a Model T Ford Van, a copy of the first motor delivery van owned by his grandfather early in the twentieth century. Villagers remember David himself delivering bread and cakes in his own distinctive green and gold van until June 3rd, 1995. He has been Chairman of the Callow End Village Hall Management Committee and is still President of the Powick and Callow End Royal British Legion. He had his very first drink in a pub at Guarlford's 'Plough and Harrow'.

Figure 8.12 The 'Village Elders' in the 'Plough and Harrow', 2006.   *(Michael Skinner).*

The Guarlford Women's Institute

Back Row - Standing

Barbara Hill; Pauline Cooper; Gail Woodhouse; Beverley Bradshaw; Sue Orgill; Judy O'Donnell; Elizabeth Tidball; Margaretha Bruce-Morgan; Mary Burrows; Daphne Hayes; Jo Newell; Becky Hayes; Judith Knott.

Front Row - Seated

Kathy Hallam; Doreen Lloyd-Jones; Judith Ashcroft; Rosemary McCulloch; Jenny Cameron; Edna Medcalf; Pauline Jones.

This photograph was taken at the Christmas Party on December 12th 2006, in Guarlford Village Hall, where meetings of Guarlford WI have been held since November 1946. Before that the Institute met in the Rectory Room, known during the Second World War as 'The Point'.

Guarlford WI was formed in May 1941. Before that time some of the women of Guarlford had been members of Madresfield WI, which, at its inception in 1917 as one of the earliest Women's Institutes in the country, was known as 'Madresfield, Newland & Guarlford Women's Institute'. So, Guarlford is a 'daughter' Institute of Madresfield, which closed in 1993. Joan Bradshaw recalled being taken as a child in a pony and trap with her mother to a meeting of the WI at Madresfield Court.

The first President of Guarlford WI was Mrs (later Lady) Wiggin, of St Cloud, Callow End, whose husband and son once farmed Clevelode Farm. Her son Sir Jerry Wiggin, sometime MP for Weston-super-Mare, also remembered his mother taking him to meetings when he was a small child. Her grandson, Bill Wiggin, is currently Conservative MP for Leominster.

At one time winter meetings were held in the afternoons, but now meetings of the Institute are usually held on the evening of the second Tuesday of the month. There is always a warm welcome for all.

Figure 8.13 The Guarlford Women's Institute, 2006. *(Colin Lettice).*

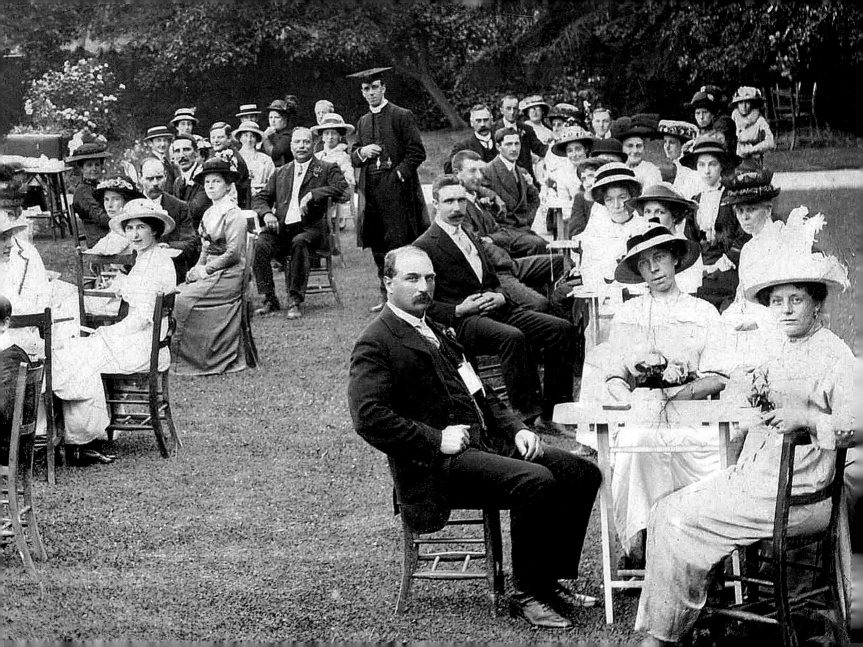

EPILOGUE

This book contains over 340 photographs of Guarlford in the twentieth century and early years of the twenty-first. Though most were taken at the time to record a moment of personal significance for an individual or family, some portray a group of villagers. One such photograph is the remarkable scene opposite in which very smartly dressed Guarlfordians pose at a whist drive presided over by the Rector, the Reverend Frederick Newson, who wears his mortar-board for the occasion. Clearly, this is a photograph from another era. Perhaps the picture also points up a contrast with more recent times in that the occasions when Guarlfordians come together for work or play are now generally far fewer, though, as this book illustrates, they do of course occur.

In the neighbourhood groups we see most of the present population of the various parts of the village. There are currently 252 on the Electoral Roll. Guarlford is a scattered settlement, with Clevelode, Rhydd, Chance Lane and the farms a little outside the main concentration of dwellings in Penny Lane, Penny Close, Rectory Lane and Bamford Close. It is quite a small settlement, too, the approximate area of the Civil Parish being eight square kilometres.

Other than extensions to existing properties and one or two barn conversions, there has been little building development in the last four decades.

Although there are inevitably many gaps in the photographic record and in what has been available to the authors, the subjects and the settings for the various photographs in and around Guarlford, as well as the story told by the text, do nevertheless help to create a larger picture of the village and its history over the last hundred or so years. No doubt like others who have compiled comparable publications, we might have wished that more information could be found to attach to particular photographs; but, of course, at the time we take photographs very few, if any of us, consider that we will find a place in a local history collection such as this one many years later.

The moment a photograph is taken its subject becomes 'history', the past. What is interesting and, for a book such as this one, essential, is the *story* that is told in retrospect of individual and shared lives at certain moments in one particular place. Cumulatively, a

Whist Drive in the Rectory Garden, c. 1920.

larger picture is created which is likely to be of potential interest not only to anyone who lives in or has connections with, in this case, Guarlford, but also, quite importantly, to local historians more widely. The story told in pictures also, of course, leaves much room for both memory and imagination to play their part in giving additional depth and meaning to the image on the page.

Looking forward, perhaps others will take up the Guarlford story and provide a further picture of the local scene at some time in the future. Meanwhile, the authors of this book and its predecessor, *The Guarlford Story*, hope that the two books provide a vivid and informative account of life in this village during the past hundred or so momentous years of chance and change. The past, as was famously said, is another country, but it is *our* country individually and collectively. It is who we are.

Guarlford's Website at www.guarlford.org.uk is open for everyone to read and to add to the narrative of Guarlford life as it continues in the present twenty-first century.

The River Severn at Clevelode by Jane Hadley-Rober

The Malvern Hills viewed from Guarlford by Angus McCulloch.